Ready, Steady, Bake

cooking for kids and with kids

Ready, Steady, Bake

cooking for kids and with kids

Lucy Broadhurst

MURDOCH BOOKS

contents

read this first...

Baking can be lots of fun and the best thing is that when you're done, you'll have some yummy treats to eat (and share). But before all the whisking, beating, mixing and pouring starts, there are some rules to follow. Sounds boring, but they're very important. You don't want your cherry ripple teacake to flop before you even take it out of the oven!

The first thing you need to do is read the recipe all the way through and check you have the right equipment and ingredients. Take any chilled ingredients, like butter and eggs, from the fridge and set aside on the kitchen bench to reach room temperature.

Next, line the tin(s) following the recipe instructions, or butter and dust with flour. Make sure you always use the shape and size of tin specified in the recipe because this affects the cooking time.

Before you turn on the oven, position the shelf in the centre of the oven, making sure there is enough room above it for the cake to rise (obviously you can't do this once the oven is hot). Preheat the oven to the temperature stated.

Even though you might be eager to start mixing, you need to weigh and measure all the ingredients properly, either with scales or cup measures.

Eggs or egg yolks should always be added to a cake mixture one at a time, beating well after you add each egg. When whisking egg whites, make sure the bowl and beaters (or whisk) are clean and dry before you start — just a hint of grease and the egg whites won't whisk properly.

Dry ingredients should always be folded into a whisked egg and sugar mixture with a large metal spoon. Fold gently from the centre of the bowl outwards. Fold whisked egg whites into the other ingredients (not the other way round).

Spoon thick cake batters into the prepared tin and carefully pour thinner batters. If necessary, smooth the surface of the batter with a spatula to ensure even cooking and browning.

All these tips should help you with your next baking adventure. The only really hard bit is deciding what to make!

Measuring up

Careful measuring of your ingredients makes for a successful recipe. You will need a set of dry measuring cups, which usually come in a set of four: a 250 ml (9 fl oz/1 cup) measure, 125 ml (4 fl oz/1/2 cup), 80 ml (2 1/2 fl oz/1/3 cup), and 60 ml (2 fl oz/1/4 cup) measure. These are used to measure ingredients such as flour and sugar. You will also need a liquid measuring cup that usually has a lip for pouring and lines on the side that mark liquid measures. Measuring spoons will also be needed to measure small amounts. They are marked and measure 1 tablespoon, 1 teaspoon, 1/2 teaspoon and 1/4 teaspoon.

Liquid measures

To measure a liquid ingredient, place the liquid measuring cup on the bench, add some of the liquid and bend down so that your eyes are level with the measurement marks. Check to see if you have enough liquid; if necessary pour in a little more. If you have too much liquid pour out the extra.

Dry measures

Use the correct size measuring cup as stated in the recipe. Spoon the dry ingredients into the measuring cup and level it off with a metal spatula. Cup and spoon measures should always be flat, not heaped.

Hygiene and safety

1. Always ask an adult for permission before you start to cook. And always ask for help if you are not confident with chopping or handling hot cake tins.

2. Before you start, wash your hands well with soap and water, tie back long hair and wear an apron to protect your clothes.

3. When you're cooking on the stovetop, turn pan handles to the side so there's no danger of knocking them as you walk past. When you're stirring, hold the pan handle firmly.

4. Never use electrical appliances near water. Always have dry hands before you start to use any appliance. Once you've finished using an appliance, switch it off at the powerpoint and remove the plug from the wall before cleaning it.

5. Always use thick, dry oven gloves when you're getting things out of the oven.

6. Remember to turn off the oven, the hotplate or gas ring when you have finished using it.

7. Wash up as you go along. This will save hours of cleaning at the end and will keep your work space clear.

sugar and spice

shortbreads

MAKES 16

250 g (9 oz/2 cups) plain (all-purpose) flour

2 tablespoons rice flour

115 (4 oz/1/2 cup) caster (superfine) sugar

250 g (9 oz) unsalted butter, chopped

1. Preheat the oven to 160°C (315°F/Gas 2–3). Lightly grease two baking trays.
2. Sift the flours together into a large bowl and mix in the sugar. Rub in the butter using your fingertips. Turn out onto a floured surface and knead gently.
3. Press out into a round about 1 cm (1/2 inch) thick. Cut out squares with a 7.5 cm (2 3/4 inch) square cutter, or any shaped cutters you have.
4. Bake for 25–30 minutes, or until lightly golden. Leave to cool on the trays for 5 minutes, then put on a wire rack to cool completely.

lemon stars

MAKES ABOUT 22

125 g (4 1/2 oz) unsalted butter, cubed and softened

125 g (4 1/2 oz/1/2 cup) caster (superfine) sugar

2 egg yolks

2 teaspoons finely grated lemon zest

155 g (5 1/2 oz/1 1/4 cups) plain (all-purpose) flour

110 g (3 3/4 oz/3/4 cup) coarse cornmeal

icing (confectioners') sugar, to dust

1. Preheat the oven to 160°C (315°F/Gas 2–3). Line a baking tray with baking paper.
2. Beat the butter and sugar using electric beaters until creamy. Mix in the egg yolks, lemon zest, flour and cornmeal until it becomes a ball of soft dough.
3. Roll out on a lightly floured surface to 1 cm (1/2 inch) thick. Cut out stars using a 3 cm (1 1/4 inch) star-shaped cutter.
4. Bake for 15–20 minutes, or until lightly golden. Cool on a wire rack, then dust with the icing sugar.

finger buns

MAKES 12

500 g (1 lb 2 oz/4 cups) plain (all-purpose) flour

35 g (1 1/4 oz/1/3 cup) milk powder

1 tablespoon dried yeast

115 g (4 oz/1/2 cup) caster (superfine) sugar

60 g (2 1/4 oz/1/2 cup) sultanas (golden raisins)

60 g (2 1/4 oz) unsalted butter, melted

1 egg, lightly beaten

1 egg yolk, extra, to glaze

glace icing (frosting)

155 g (5 1/2 oz/1 1/4 cups) icing (confectioners') sugar

20 g (3/4 oz) unsalted butter, melted

pink food colouring

1 Mix 375 g (13 oz/3 cups) of the flour with the milk powder, yeast, sugar, sultanas and 1/2 teaspoon salt in a large bowl. Make a well in the centre.

2 Combine the butter, egg and 250 ml (9 fl oz/1 cup) warm water and add to the flour. Stir for 2 minutes.

3 Turn out onto a floured surface. Knead for 10 minutes, or until smooth. Place in an oiled bowl and brush with oil. Cover with plastic wrap and leave for 1 hour.

4 Grease two large baking trays. Preheat the oven to 180°C (350°F/Gas 4). Knead the dough for 1 minute. Divide into 12 pieces. Shape each into a 15 cm (6 inch) long oval. Put on the trays 5 cm (2 inches) apart. Cover with plastic wrap and set aside for 20 minutes.

5 Mix the extra egg yolk with 1 1/2 teaspoons water and brush over the dough. Bake for 12–15 minutes, or until golden. Transfer to a wire rack to cool.

6 To make the icing (frosting), mix the icing sugar, 2–3 teaspoons water and the butter until smooth. Add the food colouring and spread over the buns.

cornflake cookies

MAKES 36

125 g ($4^1/_2$ oz) unsalted butter, softened

165 g ($5^3/_4$ oz/$^3/_4$ cup) sugar

2 eggs, lightly beaten

1 teaspoon vanilla extract

2 tablespoons currants

135 g ($4^3/_4$ oz/$1^1/_2$ cups) desiccated coconut

$^1/_2$ teaspoon bicarbonate of soda (baking soda)

$^1/_2$ teaspoon baking powder

250 g (9 oz/2 cups) plain (all-purpose) flour

75 g ($2^1/_2$ oz/$2^1/_2$ cups) cornflakes, lightly crushed

1. Preheat the oven to 180°C (350°F/Gas 4). Line two baking trays with baking paper.
2. Cream the butter and sugar using electric beaters until light and fluffy. Gradually add the egg, beating thoroughly after each addition. Add the vanilla and beat until combined.
3. Transfer the mixture to a large bowl and stir in the currants and coconut. Fold in the sifted bicarbonate of soda, baking powder and flour with a metal spoon and stir until the mixture is almost smooth. Put the cornflakes in a shallow dish, then drop level tablespoons of mixture onto the cornflakes and roll into balls. Arrange on the trays, allowing room for spreading.
4. Bake for 15–20 minutes, or until crisp and golden. Cool slightly on the tray before transferring to a wire rack to cool.

sweet puff pastry twists

MAKES 24

1 teaspoon cinnamon
2 tablespoons caster (superfine) sugar
2 sheets puff pastry
milk, for brushing

1. Preheat the oven to 200°C (400°F/Gas 6). Stir the cinnamon through the caster sugar.
2. Brush the puff pastry with milk and sprinkle the cinnamon sugar over the pastry.
3. Cut the pastry into 2 cm (3/4 inch) strips. Hold the ends of each strip and twist four times.
4. Cover a baking tray with baking paper and bake a quarter of the strips for 5 minutes, or until golden, turning once. Repeat with the remaining twists.

biscuits with passionfruit icing and coconut ice topping

MAKES ABOUT 50

biscuits (cookies)

125 g (4 1/2 oz) unsalted butter, cubed

125 g (4 1/2 oz/1/2 cup) caster (superfine) sugar

1 egg

1/4 teaspoon vanilla extract

125 g (4 1/2 oz/1 cup) plain (all-purpose) flour

125 g (4 1/2 oz/1 cup) self-raising flour

passionfruit glacé icing (frosting)

155 g (5 1/2 oz/1 1/4 cups) sifted icing (confectioners') sugar

2 tablespoons fresh passionfruit pulp

coconut ice topping

155 g (5 1/2 oz) icing (confectioners') sugar

1 tablespoon unsalted butter, softened

45 g (1 1/2 oz) desiccated coconut

1/2 teaspoon vanilla extract

few drops pink food colouring

1. Preheat the oven to 160°C (315°F/ Gas 2–3). Line a baking tray with baking paper.
2. To make the biscuits, beat together the butter and caster sugar until creamy. Add the egg and vanilla extract and beat well. Sift the plain flour and self-raising flour and fold in to form a soft dough.
3. Turn out onto a sheet of baking paper, cover with another sheet and roll out to 5 mm (1/4 inch) thick.
4. Using biscuit cutters, cut out assorted shapes and place on the tray. Bake in batches for 10–15 minutes, or until lightly golden.
5. Cool on a wire rack, then spread with your choice of topping.
6. To make the passionfruit icing, mix the icing sugar and fresh passionfruit pulp in a bowl. Stir over a saucepan of simmering water until smooth and glossy.
7. To make the coconut ice topping, mix the sifted icing sugar, butter, coconut, vanilla extract and food colouring in a bowl. Add 6–8 teaspoons of boiling water to make a thick, spreadable mixture.

Note: You can use these as toppings or to sandwich two biscuits together.

coconut jam slice

MAKES 20

125 g (4½ oz/1 cup) plain (all-purpose) flour
60 g (2¼ oz/½ cup) self-raising flour
150 g (5½ oz) unsalted butter, cubed
60 g (2¼ oz/½ cup) icing (confectioners') sugar
1 egg yolk
160 g (5¾ oz/½ cup) strawberry jam
125 g (4½ oz) caster (superfine) sugar
3 eggs
270 g (9½ oz/3 cups) desiccated coconut

1. Preheat the oven to 180°C (350°F/Gas 4). Lightly grease a shallow 23 cm (9 inch) square tin and line with baking paper, leaving the paper hanging over on two opposite sides.
2. Put the flour and icing sugar in a bowl and rub in the butter with your fingertips until the mixture is crumbly. Mix in the egg yolk and gather together.
3. Press the dough into the tin and refrigerate for 10 minutes. Bake for 15 minutes, or until golden brown. Allow to cool, then spread the jam evenly over the pastry.
4. Beat the caster sugar and eggs together until creamy, then stir in the coconut. Spread the mixture over the jam, gently pressing down with the back of a spoon.
5. Bake for 25–30 minutes, or until lightly golden. Leave to cool in the tin, then lift the slice out, using the paper as handles. Cut the slice into pieces.

Note: Store in an airtight container for up to 4 days.

pear turnovers

MAKES 12

- 10 g (1/4 oz) butter
- 140 g (5 oz) drained tinned pear pieces
- 1 teaspoon soft brown sugar
- pinch of cinnamon
- 1 sheet of puff pastry
- 1 egg, beaten
- sugar, to sprinkle
- thick (double/heavy) cream, to serve

1. Preheat the oven to 200°C (400°F/Gas 6). Lightly grease a baking tray.
2. Melt the butter in a small frying pan. Add the pear pieces, brown sugar and cinnamon and cook for 2–3 minutes, or until slightly caramelised.
3. Cut twelve 6.5 cm (2 1/2 inch) circles from the puff pastry.
4. Place 1 teaspoon of the pear mixture in the centre of each circle. Brush the edges with the beaten egg, fold over and seal with a fork.
5. Place on the prepared tray, brush with beaten egg and then sprinkle with sugar.
6. Bake for 15 minutes, or until golden. Serve with thick cream.

biscuits with marshmallow filling

MAKES ABOUT 25

125 g (4 1/2 oz) unsalted butter, cubed

125 g (4 1/2 oz/1/2 cup) caster (superfine) sugar

1 egg

1/4 teaspoon vanilla extract

125 g (4 1/2 oz/1 cup) plain (all-purpose) flour

125 g (4 1/2 oz/1 cup) self-raising flour

25 large marshmallows

1 Preheat the oven to 160°C (315°F/ Gas 2–3). Line a baking tray with baking paper.

2 Beat the butter and caster sugar until creamy. Add the egg and vanilla extract and beat well. Fold in the plain flour and self-raising flour.

3 Turn the dough out onto a sheet of baking paper and cover with another sheet. Roll out to 5 mm (1/4 inch) thick. Using biscuit cutters, cut out shapes.

4 Bake in batches for 10–15 minutes, or until lightly golden. Cool on a wire rack. Place the biscuits on a baking tray with a marshmallow on top of each one. Bake in a 180°C (350°F/Gas 4) oven for 1 minute. Sandwich with another biscuit.

heart biscuits

MAKES ABOUT 20

125 g (4 1/2 oz) butter

85 g (3 oz/2/3 cup) icing (confectioners') sugar

1 egg

a few drops red food colouring

a few drops strawberry extract

a few drops vanilla extract

285 g (10 oz/2 1/4 cups) plain (all-purpose) flour

1 Preheat the oven to 180°C (350°F/Gas 4). Line two baking trays with baking paper.

2 Beat the butter and icing sugar using electric beaters until creamy. Add the egg and beat. Transfer half the mixture into another bowl. Add the food colouring and strawberry extract to the first bowl, then beat well.

3 Add vanilla extract to the second bowl and beat well. Divide the flour between each bowl and mix.

4 Roll the portions between sheets of baking paper to 5 mm (1/4 inch) thick. Cut shapes with a heart-shaped cutter. Using a smaller cutter, cut hearts from inside larger shapes. Swap inner shapes.

5 Place on the trays and bake for 10–12 minutes, or until golden. Transfer to a wire rack to cool.

berry and apple slice

MAKES 12 PIECES

150 g (5 1/2 oz) unsalted butter

320 g (11 1/4 oz/1 1/3 cups) caster (superfine) sugar

2 eggs, lightly beaten

250 g (9 oz/2 cups) self-raising flour, sifted

160 ml (5 1/4 fl oz/2/3 cup) buttermilk

1 teaspoon vanilla extract

2 large apples, peeled, quartered and cored

150 g (5 1/2 oz/1 cup) blueberries

150 g (5 1/2 oz/1 1/4 cups) blackberries or raspberries

1 Preheat the oven to 180°C (350°F/Gas 4). Lightly grease a 20 x 30 cm (8 x 12 inch) shallow baking tin. Line with baking paper, extending over the two long sides.

2 Beat the butter and sugar in a bowl using electric beaters until light and fluffy. Add the egg gradually, beating well after each addition. Stir in the flour and buttermilk and mix until smooth. Stir through the vanilla. Spread a 5 mm (1/4 inch) layer of mixture over the base of the tin.

3 Cut the apples into very thin slices and arrange on the mixture. Spoon the remaining mixture over the apple and smooth the surface.

4 Scatter with the blueberries and blackberries. Bake for 40 minutes, or until cooked and golden.

5 Cool in the tin for 30 minutes, then lift out onto a wire rack to cool. Cut into squares to serve.

monte creams

MAKES 25

125 g (4 1/2 oz) unsalted butter
115 g (4 oz/1/2 cup) caster (superfine) sugar
3 tablespoons milk
185 g (6 1/2 oz/1 1/2 cups) self-raising flour
30 g (1 oz/1/4 cup) custard powder
30 g (1 oz/1/3 cup) desiccated coconut
custard powder, extra

filling

75 g (2 3/4 oz) unsalted butter, softened
85 g (3 oz/2/3 cup) icing (confectioners') sugar
2 teaspoons milk
105 g (3 3/4 oz/1/3 cup) strawberry jam

1. Preheat the oven to 180°C (350°F/Gas 4). Line two baking trays with baking paper.
2. Cream the butter and sugar in a bowl using electric beaters until light and fluffy. Add the milk and beat until combined. Sift the flour and custard powder and add to the bowl with the coconut. Mix to form a soft dough.
3. Roll 2 teaspoons of the mixture into balls. Place on the trays and press with a fork. Dip the fork in the extra custard powder occasionally to prevent sticking.
4. Bake for 15–20 minutes, or until golden. Transfer to a wire rack to cool completely.
5. To make the filling, beat the butter and icing sugar in a bowl using electric beaters until creamy. Beat in the milk.
6. Spread one biscuit with 1/2 teaspoon of the filling and one with 1/2 teaspoon of jam, then press together.

lemon cake with crunchy topping

SERVES 8–10

250 g (9 oz) unsalted butter, softened
200 g (7 oz) caster (superfine) sugar
2 teaspoons finely grated lemon zest
4 eggs, lightly beaten
250 g (9 oz/2 cups) self-raising flour
1 teaspoon baking powder
2 tablespoons lemon juice

crunchy topping

110 g (3¾ oz/½ cup) sugar
3 tablespoons lemon juice

1. Preheat the oven to 170°C (325°F/Gas 3). Lightly grease a 22 cm (8½ inch) square cake tin. Line the base with baking paper.
2. Cream the butter and sugar in a bowl using electric beaters until light and fluffy. Add the lemon zest, then gradually add the egg, beating well after each addition.
3. Using a large metal spoon, fold in the combined sifted flour, baking powder and ¼ teaspoon salt, as well as the lemon juice. Stir until the mixture is just combined and almost smooth.
4. Spoon the mixture into the tin and smooth the surface. Bake for 1 hour 20 minutes, or until a skewer inserted into the centre of the cake comes out clean. Remove from the tin and turn out onto a wire rack.
5. To make the topping, mix together the sugar and lemon juice (do not dissolve the sugar), and quickly brush over the top of the warm cake. The juice will sink into the cake, and the sugar will form a crunchy topping. Allow to cool before serving.

passionfruit melting moments

MAKES 14

250 g (9 oz) unsalted butter, softened

40 g (1½ oz/⅓ cup) icing (confectioners') sugar

1 teaspoon vanilla extract

185 g (6½ oz/1½ cups) self-raising flour

60 g (2¼ oz/½ cup) custard powder

passionfruit filling

60 g (2¼ oz) unsalted butter

60 g (2¼ oz/½ cup) icing (confectioners') sugar

1½ tablespoons passionfruit pulp

1. Preheat the oven to 180°C (350°F/Gas 4). Line two baking trays with baking paper.
2. Beat the butter and sugar using electric beaters until light and creamy. Beat in the vanilla extract. Sift in the flour and custard powder and mix to a soft dough.
3. Roll level tablespoons of the mixture into 28 balls and place on the trays.
4. Flatten slightly with a floured fork. Bake for about 20 minutes, or until lightly golden. Allow to cool on a wire rack.
5. To make the filling, beat the butter and sugar using electric beaters until light and creamy, then beat in the passionfruit pulp.
6. Use the filling to sandwich the biscuits together. Leave to firm before serving.

vanilla glazed rings

MAKES ABOUT 40

125 g (4 1/2 oz) unsalted butter, softened
115 g (4 oz) caster (superfine) sugar
2 teaspoons vanilla extract
1 small egg, lightly beaten
250 g (9 oz/2 cups) plain (all-purpose) flour
1/2 teaspoon baking powder

icing glaze

1 egg white
3 teaspoons lemon juice
155 g (5 1/2 oz) icing (confectioners') sugar

royal icing

1 egg white
200 g (7 oz) icing (confectioners') sugar

1. Preheat the oven to 180°C (350°F/Gas 4). Lightly grease two baking trays.
2. Beat the butter, sugar and vanilla in a bowl using electric beaters. Add the egg, beating well. Sift in the flour, baking powder and a pinch of salt. Stir with a wooden spoon to form a dough.
3. Break off small pieces of dough and roll out each piece on a lightly floured work surface to form a 10 cm (4 inch) log.
4. Curl into a ring and gently press the ends together. Place on the baking trays and bake for 10–12 minutes, or until lightly golden. Allow to cool on the trays for 5 minutes, then transfer to a wire rack to cool.
5. To make the icing glaze, combine all the ingredients in a bowl. Using a clean paintbrush, brush the tops of the biscuits with the glaze and leave to set on a wire rack.
6. To make the royal icing, combine all the ingredients in a bowl. Spoon into an icing bag. Pipe the icing backwards and forwards across the biscuits to form a zigzag pattern and leave to set.

Note: The vanilla glazed rings will keep, stored in airtight container, for up to 3 days.

rhubarb and apple crumble slice

MAKES 12 PIECES

310 g (11 oz/2 1/2 cups) plain (all-purpose) flour

270 g (9 1/2 oz) unsalted butter, softened

80 g (2 3/4 oz) caster (superfine) sugar

1 egg yolk

200 g (7 oz) slivered almonds

400 g (14 oz) tinned pie apple

500 g (1 lb 2 oz) rhubarb, drained

1 teaspoon grated lemon zest

icing (confectioners') sugar, to dust

1. Preheat the oven to 180°C (350°F/Gas 4). Lightly grease a 20 x 30 cm (8 x 12 inch) baking tin. Lline with baking paper, hanging over the two long sides.
2. Put 185 g (6 1/2 oz) of flour, 145 g (5 oz) butter and 25 g (1 oz) caster sugar in a food processor and mix in short bursts until the mixture resembles fine crumbs. Add the egg yolk and 2 tablespoons cold water and mix in short bursts to combine.
3. Press into the tin and bake for 15 minutes. Allow to cool.
4. Place the remaining flour, butter, and sugar in the food processor with 150 g (5 1/2 oz) of the almonds and mix in short bursts until the almonds are chopped. Set aside 1 cup of mixture.
5. Fold the remaining crumb mixture, apple, rhubarb and lemon zest together.
6. Cover the base of the tin with the fruit. Sprinkle with the reserved crumble, then with the remaining slivered almonds.
7. Bake for 40 minutes. Leave in the tin for 5 minutes, then turn out onto a wire rack to cool. Cut into slices and dusting with icing sugar.

hummingbird cake

SERVES 8–10

2 ripe bananas, mashed

130 g (4 3/4 oz/1/2 cup) drained and crushed tinned pineapple

285 g (10 1/4 oz/1 1/4 cups) caster (superfine) sugar

210 g (7 1/2 oz/1 2/3 cups) self-raising flour

2 teaspoons ground cinnamon or mixed (pumpkin pie) spice

170 ml (5 1/2 fl oz/2/3 cup) oil

3 tablespoons pineapple juice

2 eggs

icing (frosting)

60 g (2 1/4 oz) unsalted butter, softened

125 g (4 1/2 oz/1/2 cup) cream cheese, softened

185 g (6 1/2 oz/1 1/2 cups) icing (confectioners') sugar

1–2 teaspoons lemon juice

1. Preheat the oven to 180°C (350°F/Gas 4). Lightly grease a 20 cm (8 inch) round cake tin and line with baking paper.
2. Place the banana, pineapple and sugar in a large bowl. Add the sifted flour and cinnamon or mixed spice. Stir until well combined.
3. Whisk together the oil, pineapple juice and eggs. Pour onto the banana mixture and stir until smooth.
4. Spoon the mixture into the tin and smooth the surface. Bake for 1 hour, or until a skewer inserted into the centre of the cake comes out clean. Leave in the tin for 15 minutes, then turn out onto a wire rack to cool.
5. To make the icing, beat the butter and cream cheese using electric beaters until smooth. Gradually add the icing sugar alternately with the lemon juice. Beat until thick and creamy.
6. Spread the icing thickly over the top of the cooled cake.

chocolate cheese swirls

MAKES 24 PIECES

1.25 kg (2 lb 12 oz) cream cheese, at room temperature

120 g (4 1/4 oz) ricotta cheese

3 teaspoons vanilla extract

310 g (11 oz/1 1/4 cups) caster (superfine) sugar

6 eggs

100 g (3 1/2 oz) dark chocolate, broken into pieces

1 tablespoon milk

2 teaspoons powdered drinking chocolate

75 g (2 1/2 oz) ground hazelnuts

3 teaspoons grated orange zest

50 g (1 3/4 oz) crushed amaretti biscuits

icing (confectioners') sugar, to dust

1 Preheat the oven to 170°C (325°F/Gas 3). Lightly grease a 20 x 30 cm (8 x 12 inch) shallow baking tin. Line with baking paper, extending over the two long sides.

2 Blend the cream cheese, ricotta, vanilla and sugar in a food processor until smooth. Add the eggs and process until smooth. Divide the mixture between two bowls.

3 Bring a saucepan of water to the boil and remove from the heat. Put the chocolate, milk and drinking chocolate in a heatproof bowl and place over the water. Make the bowl doesn't touch the water. Stir occasionally until melted. Cool.

4 Add to one of the bowls of cream cheese. Mix well, then stir in the hazelnuts. Pour into the tin.

5 Stir the orange zest and biscuits into the other bowl of cream cheese. Mix well, then gently spoon over the chocolate mix, covering it completely.

6 With a knife and starting in one corner, cut the orange mix down through the chocolate, bringing the chocolate up in swirls through the orange.

7 Bake for 1 hour, or until set. Cool in the tin. Lift out and cut into squares. Dust with icing sugar to serve.

spiced scrolls

MAKES 12

250 g (9 oz/2 cups) self-raising flour

pinch of salt

30 g (1 oz) butter, chopped

185 ml (6 fl oz/3/4 cup) milk or buttermilk

spice mixture

60 g (2 1/4 oz) butter

2 tablespoons brown sugar

1 teaspoon mixed spice

60 g (2 oz) chopped pecans

1. Preheat the oven to 210°C (415°F/Gas 6–7). Lightly grease a baking tray.
2. Sift the flour and salt into a large bowl. Add the butter and rub it in lightly using your fingertips until it looks like fine breadcrumbs.
3. Make a well in the centre. Add the milk or buttermilk. Mix to a soft dough, adding more liquid if needed. Roll out to a 25 x 40 cm (10 x 16 inch) rectangle.
4. To make the spice mixture, beat the butter, brown sugar and mixed spice in a small bowl using electric beaters until light and creamy.
5. Spread the mixture over the dough and sprinkle with the pecans. Roll up from the long side.
6. Use a sharp knife to cut into 3 cm (1 1/4 inch) slices. Lay the slices close together cut side up on the tray. Bake for 12 minutes, or until golden. Cool slightly, then serve.

cinnamon teacake

SERVES 8

60 g (2¼ oz) butter
115 g (4 oz/½ cup) caster (superfine) sugar
1 egg, lightly beaten
1 teaspoon vanilla extract
90 g (3¼ oz/¾ cup) self-raising flour
30 g (1 oz/¼ cup) plain (all-purpose) flour
1 teaspoon ground cinnamon
125 ml (4 fl oz/½ cup) milk

topping

1 tablespoon caster (superfine) sugar
1 teaspoon ground cinnamon
20 g (¾ oz) butter, melted

1. Preheat the oven to 180°C (350°F/Gas 4). Lightly grease a 20 cm (8 inch) round cake tin. Line the base with baking paper.
2. Beat the butter and sugar using electric beaters until light and creamy. Add the beaten egg gradually, beating well after each addition. Add the vanilla extract and beat until combined.
3. Transfer the mixture to a large bowl. Using a spoon, fold in the sifted flours and cinnamon alternately with the milk. Stir until smooth.
4. Spoon into the tin and smooth the surface. Bake for 35–40 minutes, or until a skewer comes out clean when inserted into the centre. Leave the cake in the tin for 5 minutes, then turn out onto a wire rack.
5. Combine the sugar and cinnamon. Brush the cake with the melted butter while still warm. Sprinkle the cake with the sugar and cinnamon.

cherry ripple teacake

SERVES 8–10

700 g (1 lb 9 oz) jar pitted cherries in syrup
1 tablespoon cornflour (cornstarch)
250 g (9 oz/2 cups) self-raising flour
165 g (5 3/4 oz/3/4 cup) sugar
30 g (1 oz/1/3 cup) desiccated coconut
125 g (4 1/2 oz) butter, chopped
1 egg
185 ml (6 fl oz/3/4 cup) milk

1. Preheat oven to 180°C (350°F/Gas 4). Brush a 20 cm (8 inch) spring-form cake tin with melted butter. Line the base and sides with baking paper. Lightly grease the paper.
2. Drain the cherries, keeping 125 ml (4 fl oz/1/2 cup) of the syrup. Place the cherries in a saucepan. Blend the cornflour with the cherry syrup. Add to the saucepan. Stir over low heat until the mixture boils and thickens.
3. Sift the flour into a bowl. Add the sugar, coconut and butter. Rub the butter into the flour until it is crumbly. Measure out 1/2 cup of the mixture and set aside.
4. Add the egg and milk to the bowl and stir until almost smooth. Spoon the mixture into the tin and smooth the surface.
5. Spoon the cooled cherry mixture in small mounds over the top. Sprinkle over the 1/2 cup of coconut topping.
6. Bake for 50–55 minutes, or until lightly golden. Leave in the tin for 10 minutes, then turn out onto a wire rack to cool.

upside-down banana cake

SERVES 8

- 50 g (1¾ oz) unsalted butter, melted
- 60 g (2¼ oz/⅓ cup) soft brown sugar
- 6 very ripe large bananas, halved lengthways
- 125 g (4½ oz) unsalted butter, extra, softened
- 230 g (8½ oz/1¼ cups) soft brown sugar, extra
- 2 eggs, lightly beaten
- 185 g (6½ oz/1½ cups) self-raising flour
- 1 teaspoon baking powder
- 2 large bananas, extra, mashed

1. Preheat the oven to 180°C (350°F/Gas 4). Grease and line a 20 cm (8 inch) square cake tin.
2. Pour the melted butter over the base of the tin and sprinkle with the sugar. Arrange the bananas, cut side down, over the brown sugar.
3. Beat the butter and extra brown sugar using electric beaters until light and fluffy. Add the eggs gradually, beating well after each addition.
4. Sift the flour and baking powder into a bowl, then fold into the cake mixture with the mashed banana. Carefully spread into the tin.
5. Bake for 45 minutes, or until a skewer inserted into the centre of the cake comes out clean. Turn out onto a wire rack to cool.

easy sponge cake with strawberries and cream

SERVES 6

30 g (1 oz) butter, melted

60 g ($2^{1}/_{4}$ oz/$^{1}/_{2}$ cup) plain (all-purpose) flour

60 g ($2^{1}/_{4}$ oz/$^{1}/_{2}$ cup) cornflour (cornstarch)

2 teaspoons cream of tartar

1 teaspoon bicarbonate of soda (baking soda)

4 eggs

170 g (6 oz/$^{3}/_{4}$ cup) caster (superfine) sugar

2 tablespoons hot milk

300 ml ($10^{1}/_{2}$ fl oz) pouring (whipping) cream

1 tablespoon icing (confectioners') sugar, plus extra to dust

2 tablespoons strawberry jam

500 g (1 lb 2 oz) strawberries, hulled and sliced in half

1 Preheat the oven to 180°C (350°F/Gas 4). Grease two 20 cm (8 inch) round cake tins with the melted butter. Line the bases with baking paper. Dust the sides of the tins with a little flour, shaking out any excess.

2 Sift the flour, cornflour, cream of tartar and bicarbonate of soda into a bowl, then repeat twice.

3 Whisk the eggs and sugar in a bowl for 5 minutes, or until pale and thick. Fold in the flour mixture and the hot milk until they are just combined. Do not overmix.

4 Divide the mixture evenly between the two tins. Bake for 18–20 minutes, or until golden. Leave in the tins for 5 minutes, then turn out onto a wire rack to cool.

5 Whip the cream and icing sugar in a bowl until fluffy. Place a sponge cake on a plate and spread with jam.

6 Top with half the cream and half of the strawberries.

7 Cover with the second sponge. Spread the remaining cream over the top and top with the remaining strawberries. Dust with icing sugar to serve.

5

6

7

swiss roll

SERVES 10

90 g ($3^{1}/_{4}$ oz/$^{3}/_{4}$ cup) self-raising flour

3 eggs, lightly beaten

170 g (6 oz/$^{3}/_{4}$ cup) caster (superfine) sugar

160 g ($5^{3}/_{4}$ oz/$^{1}/_{2}$ cup) strawberry jam, beaten

icing (confectioners') sugar, to dust

1 Preheat the oven to 190°C (375°F/Gas 5). Lightly grease a shallow 2 x 25 x 30 cm ($^{3}/_{4}$ x 10 x 12 inch) Swiss roll tin (jelly roll tin). Line the base with baking paper, extending over the two long sides. Sift the flour three times onto baking paper.

2 Beat the eggs in a bowl using electric beaters for 5 minutes, or until thick and pale. Add 115 g (4 oz/ $^{1}/_{2}$ cup) of the sugar gradually, beating until the mixture is pale. Transfer to a large bowl.

3 Using a metal spoon, fold in the flour quickly. Spread into the tin and smooth the surface.

4 Bake for 10–12 minutes, or until lightly golden and springy to the touch. Leave in the tin.

5 Place a tea towel on the kitchen bench. Cover with baking paper and sprinkle with the remaining caster sugar. Turn the cake out onto the baking paper.

6 Roll the cake up from the short side, rolling the paper inside the roll. Put the rolled cake on a wire rack for 5 minutes, then unroll and allow the cake to cool.

7 Spread with the jam and re-roll. Trim the ends with a knife. Sprinkle with icing sugar.

pineapple upside-down cake

SERVES 8–10

base

60 g (2$^1/_4$ oz) unsalted butter

95 g (3$^1/_4$ oz/$^1/_2$ cup) brown sugar

4 slices canned pineapple, drained and halved

12 glace cherries

cake

125 g (4$^1/_2$ oz) butter

115 g (4 oz/$^1/_2$ cup) caster (superfine) sugar

2 eggs

1 teaspoon vanilla extract

185 g (6$^1/_2$ oz/1$^1/_2$ cups) self raising flour, sifted

125 ml (4 fl oz/$^1/_2$ cup) milk

1. To prepare the base, cream the butter and sugar in a small bowl. Spread over the base of a 20 cm (8 inch) spring-form cake tin lined with baking paper.
2. Arrange the pineapple and cherries over base. Set aside.
3. To prepare the cake, preheat the oven to 180°C (350°F/Gas 4). Cream the butter and sugar until fluffy. Add the eggs one at a time, beating well after each addition. Stir in the vanilla extract.
4. Fold the flour into the creamed mixture alternately with milk, beginning and ending with flour.
5. Spread the cake mixture carefully over the base. Bake about 45–50 minutes. Cool in tin for 15 minutes, then turn out onto wire rack to cool completely.

little cakes

little jam-filled cakes

MAKES 12

- 280 g (10 oz/2 1/4 cups) self-raising flour
- 170 g (6 oz/3/4 cup) caster (superfine) sugar
- 250 ml (9 fl oz/1 cup) milk
- 2 eggs, lightly beaten
- 1/2 teaspoon natural vanilla extract
- 75 g (2 1/2 oz) unsalted butter, melted
- 80 g (2 3/4 oz/1/4 cup) strawberry jam
- 12 small strawberries, hulled
- icing (confectioners') sugar, to dust

1. Preheat the oven to 200°C (400°F/Gas 6). Grease 12 standard muffin holes.
2. Sift the flour into a bowl, add the sugar and stir to combine. Make a well in the centre.
3. Put the milk, eggs, vanilla and butter in a bowl and whisk to combine. Pour into the well and, using a metal spoon, fold the milk mixture into the flour mixture until just combined.
4. Divide three-quarters of the cake batter between the muffin holes. Top each with 1 teaspoon of the jam and cover with the remaining cake batter. Gently press a strawberry into the centre.
5. Bake for 20 minutes, or until light golden. Cool in the tin for 5 minutes, then turn out onto a wire rack to cool completely. Dust with icing sugar to serve.

Note: The cakes are best served on the day they are made.

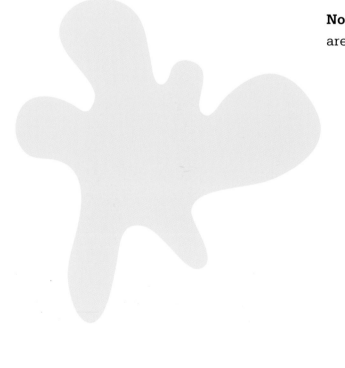

blueberry muffins

MAKES 12

375 g (13 oz/3 cups) plain (all-purpose) flour
1 tablespoon baking powder
165 g (5¾ oz/¾ cup) soft brown sugar
125 g (4½ oz) unsalted butter, melted
2 eggs, lightly beaten
250 ml (9 fl oz/1 cup) milk
185 g (6½ oz/1¼ cups) fresh or thawed frozen blueberries

1. Preheat the oven to 210°C (415°F/Gas 6–7). Grease 12 standard muffin holes.
2. Sift the flour and baking powder into a large bowl. Stir in the sugar and make a well in the centre.
3. Add the combined melted butter, eggs and and fold until just combined. Do not overmix — the batter should be lumpy. Fold in the blueberries.
4. Spoon the batter into the prepared tin. Bake for 20 minutes, or until golden brown. Cool on a wire rack.

apple and cinnamon muffins

MAKES 12

- 300 g (10 1/2 oz/2 cups) self-raising flour
- 140 g (5 oz/3/4 cup, lightly packed) soft brown sugar
- 1 teaspoon cinnamon
- 160 ml (5 1/4 fl oz/2/3 cup) milk
- 4 tablespoons canola oil
- 2 eggs, whisked
- 2 ripe apples, peeled, grated

1. Preheat the oven to 180°C (350°F/Gas 4). Lightly grease twelve 80 ml (2 1/2 fl oz/1/3 cup) muffin holes.
2. Sift the flour, sugar and cinnamon into a large bowl.
3. In a separate bowl, combine the milk, oil and eggs. Add the milk mixture and apples to the flour mixture. Mix until just combined. Spoon evenly among the muffin holes.
4. Bake for 18–20 minutes, or until lightly golden. Leave for 5 minutes, then turn out onto a wire rack to cool.

almond, berry and yoghurt muffins

MAKES 12

185g (6 1/2 oz/1 1/2 cups) plain (all-purpose) flour

3 teaspoons baking powder

115 g (4 oz/1 cup) ground almonds

185g (6 1/2 oz/3/4 cup) caster (superfine) sugar

2 eggs

125 g (4 1/2 oz) unsalted butter, melted, cooled

250g (9 oz/1 cup) plain (all-purpose) yoghurt

300 g (10 1/2 oz) blueberries or raspberries

2 tablespoons flaked almonds

1 Preheat the oven to 180°C (350°F/Gas 4). Grease 12 standard muffin holes.

2 Sift the flour and baking powder into a large bowl and stir in the ground almonds and sugar. Make a well in the centre.

3 Put the eggs, butter and yoghurt in a bowl, whisk and pour into the well. Fold gently until well combined — the batter should be lumpy.

4 Fold in the berries. Divide the mixture among the muffin holes. Top each muffin with flaked almonds.

5 Bake for 20 minutes, or until lightly golden. Cool for 5 minutes, then transfer to a wire rack.

lamingtons

MAKES 16

185 g (6½ oz/1½ cups) self-raising flour
40 g (1½ oz/⅓ cup) cornflour (cornstarch)
185 g (6½ oz) unsalted butter, softened
230 g (8½ oz/1 cup) caster (superfine) sugar
2 teaspoons natural vanilla extract
3 eggs, lightly beaten
125 ml (4 fl oz/½ cup) milk

icing (frosting)

500 g (1 lb 2 oz/4 cups) icing (confectioners') sugar
40 g (1½ oz/⅓ cup) unsweetened cocoa powder
30 g (1 oz) unsalted butter, melted
170 ml (5½ fl oz/⅔ cup) milk
270 g (9½ oz/3 cups) desiccated coconut

1 Preheat the oven to 180°C (350°F/Gas 4). Grease a shallow 23 cm (9 inch) square cake tin and line the base and sides with baking paper.

2 Sift the flour and cornflour into a bowl. Add the butter, sugar, vanilla, egg and milk. Using electric beaters, beat for 3 minutes. Pour into the tin.

3 Bake for 50–55 minutes, or until lightly golden. Leave for 3 minutes, then turn out onto a wire rack to cool.

4 Using a knife, trim the crusts from the sides. Cut the cake into 16 squares.

5 To make the icing, sift the icing sugar and cocoa into a heatproof bowl and add the butter and milk. Stand over a saucepan of simmering water and stir until the icing is smooth, then remove from the heat.

6 Place 90 g (3¼ oz/1 cup) of the coconut in a bowl. Using two forks, roll a piece of cake in chocolate icing, then hold over the bowl to allow the excess to drain.

7 Roll the cake in coconut, then place on a wire rack. Repeat with the remaining cake.

chocolate hazelnut friands

MAKES 12

185 g (6 1/2 oz) unsalted butter
6 egg whites
155 g (5 1/2 oz/1 1/4 cups) plain (all-purpose) flour
30 g (1 oz/1/4 cup) unsweetened cocoa powder
250 g (9 oz/2 cups) confectioners') sugar
200 g (7 oz) ground hazelnuts

1. Preheat the oven to 200°C (400°F/Gas 6). Grease twelve 125 ml (4 fl oz/1/2 cup) friand holes.
2. Place the butter in a small saucepan and melt over medium heat. Cook for 3–4 minutes, or until it turns a deep golden colour. Set aside to cool.
3. Lightly whisk the egg whites in a bowl until frothy. Sift the flour, cocoa powder and icing sugar into a large bowl. Stir in the ground hazelnuts.
4. Make a well in the centre. Add the egg whites and butter and mix until combined. Spoon the mixture into the friand holes until three-quarters filled.
5. Bake for 20–25 minutes, or until a skewer inserted into the centre comes out clean. Leave in the tin for a few minutes, then cool on a wire rack.

madeleines

MAKES 14 (OR 30 SMALL ONES)

3 eggs
100 g (3 1/2 oz/1/2 cup) caster (superfine) sugar
150 g (5 1/2 oz/1 1/4 cups) plain (all-purpose) flour
100 g (3 1/2 oz) unsalted butter, melted
grated zest of 1 lemon and 1 orange

1. Preheat the oven to 200°C (400°F/Gas 6). Brush a tray of madeleine moulds with melted butter and coat with flour, then tap the tray to remove the excess flour.
2. Whisk the eggs and sugar until the mixture is thick and pale and the whisk leaves a trail when lifted.
3. Gently fold in the flour, then the melted butter and grated lemon and orange zest. Spoon into the moulds, leaving a little room for rising.
4. Bake for 12 minutes (small madeleines will only need 7 minutes), or until very lightly golden. Turn out onto a wire rack to cool.

flourless chocolate cakes

MAKES 8

250 g (9 oz) dark chocolate, chopped
100 g (3 1/2 oz) caster (superfine) sugar
100 g (3 1/2 oz) unsalted butter, cubed
125 g (4 1/2 oz) ground hazelnuts
5 eggs, separated
icing (confectioners') sugar, to dust

1. Preheat the oven to 180°C (350°F/Gas 4). Grease eight 125 ml (4 fl oz/1/2 cup) mini flower-shaped tins and line the bases with baking paper.
2. Place the chocolate, sugar and butter in a heatproof bowl. Sit the bowl over a saucepan of simmering water, making sure the base of the bowl does not touch the water. Stir occasionally. Remove from the heat and stir well.
3. Transfer the chocolate mixture to a large bowl. Stir in the hazelnuts, then beat in the egg yolks, one at a time, mixing well after each addition.
4. In a separate bowl, whisk the egg whites until stiff peaks form. Gently fold into the chocolate using a metal spoon or spatula. Pour the mixture into the tin
5. Bake for 30–40 minutes, or until a skewer inserted into the centre of the cake comes out clean. Leave to cool completely in the tin, then turn out and dust with icing sugar.

lemon coconut cakes

MAKES 5

185 g (6 1/2 oz/1 1/2 cups) self-raising flour
45 g (1 3/4 oz/1/2 cup) desiccated coconut
1 tablespoon grated lemon zest
230 g (8 1/2 oz/1 cup) caster (superfine) sugar
125 g (4 1/2 oz) unsalted butter, melted
2 eggs
250 ml (9 fl oz/1 cup) milk

coconut icing (frosting)

185 g (6 1/2 oz/1 1/2 cups) icing (confectioners') sugar, sifted
90 g (3 1/4 oz/1 cup) desiccated coconut, plus extra, to decorate
1/2 teaspoon grated lemon zest
3 tablespoons lemon juice

1. Preheat the oven to 180°C (350°F/Gas 4). Lightly grease five 175 ml (5 1/2 fl oz) mini bundt tins.
2. Sift the flour into a large bowl and add the coconut, lemon zest, sugar, butter, eggs and milk. Mix well with a wooden spoon until smooth. Pour into the tins and smooth the surface.
3. Bake for 20–25 minutes, or until lightly golden. Leave the cakes in the tins for 5 minutes, then turn out onto a wire rack to cool completely.
4. To make the icing, combine the icing sugar and coconut in a bowl. Add the lemon zest and lemon juice.
5. Top the cakes with the icing and decorate with the extra coconut.

raspberry and passionfruit cakes

MAKES 6

- 30 g (1 oz/1/4 cup) plain (all-purpose) flour
- 90 g (3 1/4 oz/3/4 cup) self-raising flour
- 140 g (4 2/3 oz/3/4 cup) ground almonds
- 185 g (6 1/2 oz) unsalted butter
- 250 g (9 oz/1 cup) caster (superfine) sugar
- 125 g (4 1/2 oz/1/2 cup) fresh passionfruit pulp
- 2 teaspoons vanilla extract
- 2 eggs
- 125 g (4 1/2 oz/1 cup) frozen or fresh raspberries
- icing (confectioners') sugar, to dust

1. Preheat the oven to 180°C (350°F/Gas 4). Grease six 160 ml (5 1/4 fl oz) mini heart-shaped tins.
2. Combine the plain flour, self-raising flour and ground almonds in a large bowl. Make a well in the centre.
3. Put the butter, sugar, pulp and vanilla extract in a saucepan. Stir over low heat until the butter has melted and the mixture is smooth.
4. Whisk the butter mixture into the dry ingredients. Whisk in the eggs until smooth.
5. Pour the mixture into the tins. Drop the raspberries on top, pushing them just below the surface.
6. Bake for 25 minutes, or until lightly golden. Set aside for 10 minutes, then turn out onto a wire rack to cool. Dust with icing sugar to serve.

vanilla coconut cupcakes

MAKES 12

150 g (5 1/2 oz) unsalted butter, cut into cubes

115 g (4 oz/1/2 cup) caster (superfine) sugar

2 teaspoons vanilla extract

2 eggs

185 g (6 1/2 oz/1 1/2 cups) plain (all-purpose) flour

1 teaspoon baking powder

45 g (1 1/2 oz/1/2 cup) desiccated coconut

125 ml (4 fl oz/1/2 cup) milk

vanilla icing (frosting)

60 g (2 1/4 oz/1 cup) flaked coconut

20 g (3/4 oz) unsalted butter, cut into cubes

2 teaspoons vanilla extract

185 g (6 1/2 oz/1 1/2 cups) icing (confectioners') sugar, sifted

1 Preheat the oven to 180°C (350°F/Gas 4). Line 12 standard muffin holes with paper cases.

2 Put the butter, sugar and vanilla extract in a bowl and beat using electric beaters for 2–3 minutes, or until thick and creamy. Add the eggs, one at a time, and beat until well combined.

3 Sift together the flour and baking powder. Add to the mixture gradually. Stir in the desiccated coconut and the milk. Put spoonfuls evenly into the paper cases.

4 Bake for 18–20 minutes, or until golden brown. Cool on a wire rack.

5 To make the vanilla icing, spread the flaked coconut on a tray and lightly toast for 2–3 minutes in the oven. Put the butter in a small bowl and pour over 2 teaspoons of hot water to soften the butter. Add the vanilla extract. Put the icing sugar in a bowl, add the butter mixture and mix together until smooth, adding a little more water if neeeded.

6 Use a small spatula to spread the cakes with the icing and dip each into the coconut flakes.

individual milk chocolate cakes

MAKES 6

75 g (2¾ oz) unsalted butter
75 g (2¾ oz) milk chocolate, chopped
80 g (2¾ oz/⅓ cup) brown sugar
2 eggs, lightly beaten
60 g (2¼ oz/½ cup) self-raising flour, sifted
silver cachous, to decorate

ganache

80 g (2¾ oz) milk chocolate, chopped
2 tablespoons thick (double/heavy) cream

1. Preheat the oven to 160°C (315°F/Gas 2–3). Line a flat-bottomed 6-hole cupcake tray with paper patty cases.
2. Put the butter and chocolate in a heatproof bowl and place over a saucepan of simmering water, making sure the base of the bowl doesn't touch the water. Stir until melted. Remove from the heat, add the sugar and egg and mix. Stir in the flour.
3. Transfer the mixture to a measuring jug and pour into the patty cases.
4. Bake for 20–25 minutes, or until cooked. Leave in the tin for 10 minutes, then transfer to a wire rack to cool.
5. To make the ganache, place the chocolate and cream in a heatproof bowl. Place over a saucepan of simmering water. Stir until melted. Allow to cool for about 8 minutes, or until thickened slightly.
6. Spread a heaped teaspoon of ganache over the top of each cake. Decorate with silver cachous.

lemon meringue muffins

MAKES 12

- 330 g ($11\frac{3}{4}$ oz/$1\frac{3}{4}$ cups) self-raising flour
- 185 g ($6\frac{1}{2}$ oz/$\frac{3}{4}$ cup) caster (superfine) sugar
- 1 egg
- 1 egg yolk
- 170 ml ($5\frac{1}{2}$ fl oz/$\frac{2}{3}$ cup) milk
- $\frac{1}{2}$ teaspoon vanilla extract
- 90 g ($3\frac{1}{4}$ oz) unsalted butter, melted and cooled
- 200 g (7 oz/$\frac{2}{3}$ cup) ready-made lemon curd
- 3 egg whites

1. Preheat the oven to 200°C (400°F/Gas 6). Grease 12 standard muffin holes.
2. Sift the flour into a large bowl and stir in 60 g ($2\frac{1}{4}$ oz/$\frac{1}{4}$ cup) of the caster sugar. Make a well in the centre.
3. Put a pinch of salt, the egg and egg yolk in a bowl and beat together. Stir in the milk, vanilla and butter. Pour into the well. Fold until just combined.
4. Divide the muffin mixture among the holes. Bake for 15 minutes. Cool in the tin for 10 minutes.
5. Hollow out the centre of each muffin with a knife.
6. Spoon the lemon curd into the muffin holes.
7. Whisk the egg whites until firm peaks form. Add the remaining sugar, beating well after each addition.
8. Reduce the oven to 150°C (300°F/Gas 2). Put a heaped tablespoon of meringue on top of each muffin. Sprinkle over a little caster sugar. Bake for 5–7 minutes, or until crisp. Cool in the tin for 10 minutes, then transfer to a wire rack.

pear and muesli muffins

MAKES 12

225 g (8 oz/1 1/2 cups) toasted muesli
1 tablespoon plain (all-purpose) flour
125 g (4 1/2 oz/1/2 cup) caster (superfine) sugar
90 g (3 1/4 oz) unsalted butter, melted
100 g (3 1/2 oz/1/2 cup) chopped dried pears
125 ml (4 fl oz/1/2 cup) orange juice
1 tablespoon finely grated orange zest
250 g (9 oz/2 cups) self-raising flour
1/2 teaspoon baking powder
250 ml (9 fl oz/1 cup) buttermilk
3 tablespoons milk
90 g (3 1/4 oz/1/4 cup) honey

1. To make the topping, place 75 g (2 1/2 oz/1/2 cup) of the muesli, the plain flour and half the sugar in a small bowl and mix in 2 tablespoons of the butter.
2. Preheat the oven to 200°C (400°F/Gas 6). Grease 12 standard muffin holes. Put the pears in a bowl and add the orange juice and zest. Leave for 10 minutes.
3. Sift the self-raising flour and baking powder into the bowl with the pears. Add the remaining muesli and sugar. Make a well in the centre.
4. Whisk the buttermilk and milk together and add to the pear mixture. Combine the honey and remaining butter, then add to the pear mixture. Mix well.
5. Divide the batter among the muffin holes, then sprinkle on the topping. Bake for 25–30 minutes, or until cooked. Cool briefly, then transfer to a wire rack.

wholemeal apricot rock cakes

MAKES 20

225 g (8 oz/1 1/2 cups) stoneground wholemeal self-raising flour

1/2 teaspoons baking powder

1 1/2 teaspoons ground cinnamon

55 g (2 oz/1/2 cup) ground almonds

80 g (2 3/4 oz/1/3 cup) raw sugar

185 g (6 1/2 oz/1 cup) dried apricots, chopped

1 tablespoon sunflower or pepitas (pumpkin seeds)

90 g (3 1/4 oz) butter, melted

1 egg, lightly beaten

3 tablespoons buttermilk

1. Preheat the oven to 180°C (350°F/Gas 4). Line a large baking tray with baking paper.
2. Sift the flour, baking powder and cinnamon into a large bowl, then return any husks to the bowl. Stir in the ground almonds, raw sugar, apricots and seeds. Make a well in the centre.
3. Combine the butter, egg and buttermilk in a small bowl. Pour into the well in the dry ingredients and mix briefly with a fork until just combined.
4. Using 1 heaped tablespoon of batter at a time, put spoonfuls onto the tray, forming a little mound.
5. Bake for 15–20 minutes, or until cooked. Leave on the tray for 2–3 minutes, then transfer to a wire rack to cool completely.

banana muffins with caramel syrup

MAKES 12

250 g (9 oz/2 cups) self-raising flour

125 g ($4^{1}/_{2}$ oz/$^{1}/_{2}$ cup) caster (superfine) sugar

250 ml (9 fl oz/1 cup) milk

1 egg

2 teaspoons vanilla extract

75 g ($2^{1}/_{2}$ oz) unsalted butter, melted and cooled

240 g ($8^{1}/_{2}$ oz/1 cup) mashed banana

300 g ($10^{1}/_{2}$ oz) sugar

1 Preheat the oven to 200°C (400°F/Gas 6). Grease 12 standard muffin holes.

2 Sift the flour into a bowl and stir in the caster sugar. Make a well in the centre.

3 Put the milk, egg and vanilla in a bowl. Whisk and pour into the well.

4 Add the butter and banana. Fold until combined—the batter should be lumpy.

5 Divide among the muffin holes. Bake for about 20–25 minutes, or until lightly golden.

6 To make the syrup, put the sugar and about 100 ml ($3^{1}/_{2}$ fl oz) of water in a small saucepan over medium heat and stir until the sugar dissolves. Increase the heat and cook for 8 minutes, or until golden. Remove from the heat and 4 tablespoons of water (careful—it will spit). Stir the water into the caramel until smooth.

7 Cool in the tin for 5 minutes, then transfer to a wire rack. Drizzle with the syrup.

strawberry and blueberry shortcakes

MAKES 4

shortcake

90 g (3¼ oz) butter
60 g (2¼ oz) sugar
1 egg
140 g (5 oz) plain (all-purpose) flour
2 teaspoons baking powder
a pinch of salt
4 tablespoons milk
whipped cream, to serve
250 g (9 oz) strawberries, quartered
150 g (5½ oz) blueberries
icing (confectioners') sugar, to dust

1. Preheat the oven to 180°C (350°F/Gas 4). Cream the butter with the sugar until light and creamy. Add the egg and mix well.
2. Sift in the flour, baking powder and salt, then add the milk. Fold well.
3. Roll out to 2 cm (¾ inch) thick on a well-floured surface. Cut into circles using 7.5 cm (3 inch) round cutter. Put the circles on a greased baking tray and bake for 20 minutes.
4. Cool slightly, then split and fill with cream and strawberries and blueberries. Dust with icing sugar to serve.

strawberry muffins

MAKES 18

375 g (13 oz/3 cups) plain (all-purpose) flour
110 g (3¾ oz/½ cup) sugar
1 tablespoon baking powder
95 g (3¼ oz/½ cup) brown sugar
125 g (4½ oz) unsalted butter, melted
3 eggs
250 ml (9 fl oz/1 cup) milk
225 g (8 oz/1½ cups) strawberries, chopped

1. Preheat the oven to 200°C (400°F/Gas 6). Lightly grease 18 standard muffin holes.
2. Sift the flour, sugar and baking powder into a bowl. Stir in the brown sugar.
3. Combine the melted butter, eggs and milk. Stir into the dry ingredients until just blended.
4. Fold in the berries very lightly. Spoon into the muffin holes until three-quarters full.
5. Bake for 20 minutes, or until lightly golden. Serve hot with butter.

individual white chocolate chip cakes

MAKES 12

125 g (4 1/2 oz) unsalted butter, softened
185 g (6 1/2 oz/3/4 cup) caster (superfine) sugar
2 eggs, lightly beaten
1 teaspoon vanilla extract
250 g (9 oz/2 cups) self-raising flour, sifted
125 ml (4 fl oz/1/2 cup) buttermilk
250 g (9 oz) white chocolate chips
white chocolate, shaved, to decorate

white chocolate cream cheese icing (frosting)

100 g (3 1/2 oz) white chocolate
3 tablespoons thick (double/heavy) cream
200 g (7 oz/3/4 cup) cream cheese, softened
40 g (1 1/2 oz/1/3 cup) icing (confectioners') sugar

1 Preheat the oven to 170°C (325°F/Gas 3). Grease 12 standard muffin holes.

2 Beat the butter and sugar in a large bowl using electric beaters until pale and creamy. Gradually add the egg, beating well after each addition. Add the vanilla extract and beat until combined.

3 Fold in the flour alternately with the buttermilk, then fold in the chocolate chips.

4 Spoon into the muffin holes until three-quarters full. Bake for 20 minutes, or until lightly golden. Leave in the tins for 5 minutes, then turn out onto a wire rack to cool.

5 To make the icing, melt the chocolate and cream in a small saucepan over low heat until smooth. Cool slightly, then add to the cream cheese and icing sugar and beat until smooth.

6 Spread the icing over the cakes and top with white chocolate shavings.

chocolate muffins

MAKES 12

- 310 g (11 oz/2 1/2 cups) self-raising flour
- 40 g (1 1/2 oz/1/3 cup) unsweetened cocoa powder
- 1/2 teaspoon bicarbonate of soda (baking soda)
- 180 g (6 oz/2/3 cup) caster (superfine) sugar
- 375 ml (12 fl oz/1 1/2 cups) buttermilk
- 2 eggs
- 150 g (5 1/2 oz) unsalted butter, melted and cooled
- 60 g (2 1/4 oz) chocolate, grated

1. Preheat the oven to 200°C (400°F/Gas 6). Grease 12 standard muffin holes.
2. Sift the flour, cocoa and bicarbonate of soda into a bowl and add the sugar. Make a well in the centre.
3. Whisk the buttermilk and eggs together and pour into the well. Add the butter and fold gently with a metal spoon until just combined. Do not overmix. Fill each muffin hole about three-quarters full.
4. Bake for 20–25 minutes, or until the muffins are risen. Cool for 2 minutes, then transfer to a wire rack. Sprinkle the grated chocolate on top while still warm.

rhubarb and custard muffins

MAKES 12

- 185 g (6 1/2 oz/3/4 cup) caster (superfine) sugar
- 300 g (10 1/2 oz) chopped rhubarb
- 280 g (2 1/4 cups) self-raising flour
- 90 g (3 1/4 oz/3/4 cup) custard powder
- 125 g (4 1/2 oz/1/2 cup) caster (superfine) sugar
- 1 egg
- 30 g (1 oz) unsalted butter, melted and cooled
- 250 ml (9 fl oz/1 cup) skim milk

1. Preheat the oven to 200°C (400°F/Gas 6). Grease 12 standard muffin holes.
2. Combine the caster sugar and 250 ml (9 fl oz/1 cup) of water in a saucepan and stir over medium heat. Add the rhubarb and cook over low heat for 2 minutes, or until tender. Transfer to a bowl and cool. Drain, being careful not to break up the rhubarb.
3. Sift the self-raising flour and custard powder into a bowl. Stir in the caster sugar.
4. Combine the egg, butter and milk and add to the dry ingredients. Fold until combined. Fold in the rhubarb.
5. Divide the mixture among the muffin holes. Sprinkle with sugar and bake for 20 minutes, or until golden. Cool for 5 minutes, then transfer to a wire rack.

yoghurt banana cakes with honey icing

MAKES 6

180 g (6 oz) unsalted butter, softened

90 g (3 1/4 oz/1/4 cup) honey

230 g (8 oz/1 cup) caster (superfine) sugar

1 1/2 teaspoons vanilla extract

3 eggs

360 g (12 3/4 oz/1 1/2 cups) mashed ripe banana (about 4 bananas)

185 g (6 1/2 oz/3/4 cup) plain yoghurt

1/2 teaspoon bicarbonate of soda (baking soda)

375 g (13 oz/3 cups) self-raising flour, sifted

honey icing (frosting)

125 g (4 1/2 oz) unsalted butter

3 tablespoons honey

125 g (4 1/2 oz/1 cup) icing (confectioners') sugar

1 tablespoon milk

1. Preheat the oven to 180°C (350°F/Gas 4). Lightly grease six 10 cm (4 inch) round cake tins and line the bases with baking paper.
2. Cream the butter, honey, sugar and vanilla in a bowl using electric beaters until fluffy. Add the eggs one at a time, beating well after each addition, then beat in the banana.
3. Combine the yoghurt and bicarbonate of soda in a small bowl. Fold the flour alternately with the yoghurt into the banana mixture. Divide the mixture evenly between the tins, smoothing the tops.
4. Bake for 50–60 minutes, or until a skewer inserted into the centre of a cake comes out clean. Cool in the tins for 5 minutes, then turn out onto a wire rack.
5. To make the honey icing, cream the butter and honey in a small bowl using electric beaters until fluffy. Gradually add the icing sugar alternately with the milk, beating well until the mixture is very pale. When the cakes are cold, divide the honey icing between the tops, spreading the icing to form rough peaks.

Note: These cakes will keep, stored in an airtight container, for up to 4 days. Un-iced cakes can be frozen for up to 3 months.

berry cheesecake muffins

MAKES 6

215 g (7½ oz/1¾ cups) self-raising flour

2 eggs, lightly beaten

3 tablespoons oil

2 tablespoons raspberry jam

60 g (2¼ oz/¼ cup) mixed berry yoghurt

125 g (4½ oz/½ cup) caster (superfine) sugar

60 g (2¼ oz) cream cheese

1 tablespoon raspberry jam, extra, for filling

icing (confectioners') sugar, sifted, to dust

1. Preheat the oven to 180°C (350°F/Gas 4). Lightly grease six standard muffin holes.
2. Sift the flour into a large bowl and make a well in the centre. Place the eggs, oil, jam, yoghurt and sugar in a separate bowl and combine. Add to the sifted flour. Mix the batter until just combined.
3. Spoon three-quarters of the mixture into the muffin holes. Cut the cream cheese into six equal portions and place a portion on the centre of each muffin. Spread the tops with jam and cover with remaining muffin batter.
4. Bake for 30 minutes, or until lightly golden. Turn out onto a wire rack to cool. Dust with icing sugar to serve.

Note: These muffins are best eaten as soon as they are cool enough.

mini mango cakes with lime syrup

MAKES 4

425 g (15 oz) tinned mango slices in syrup, drained

90 g (3¼ oz) unsalted butter, softened

185 g (6½ oz/¾ cup) caster (superfine) sugar

2 eggs, lightly beaten

60 g (2¼ oz/½ cup) self-raising flour

2 tablespoons ground almonds

2 tablespoons coconut milk

2 tablespoons lime juice

1 Preheat the oven to 200°C (400°F/Gas 6). Grease four standard muffin holes and line with mango slices.

2 Beat the butter and 125 g (4 fl oz/½ cup) of the sugar in a bowl using electric beaters until creamy. Gradually add the egg, beating well after each addition. Fold in the sifted flour, then add the almonds and coconut milk. Spoon into the muffin holes.

3 Bake for 25 minutes, or until lightly golden. Once cool, pierce holes in each cake with a skewer.

4 To make the syrup, put the lime juice, the remaining sugar and 125 ml (4 fl oz/½ cup) of water in a small saucepan and stir over low heat until the sugar dissolves. Increase the heat and simmer for 10 minutes.

5 Drizzle the syrup over the top. Stand for 5 minutes to soak up the liquid. Turn out and serve.

sand cakes with passionfruit cream cheese icing

MAKES 6

185 g (6½ oz) unsalted butter, softened
2 teaspoons vanilla extract
250 g (9 oz/1 cup) caster (superfine) sugar
3 eggs
185 g (6½ oz/1½ cups) self-raising flour
60 g (2¼ oz/⅓ cup) rice flour
4 tablespoons milk

passionfruit cream cheese icing (frosting)

100 g (3⅓ oz) cream cheese, at room temperature
90 g (3¼ oz/¾ cup) icing (confectioners') sugar, sifted
1–2 tablespoons passionfruit pulp

1. Preheat the oven to 180°C (350°F/ Gas 4). Lightly grease six standard muffin holes and line the bases with baking paper.
2. Beat the butter, vanilla extract, sugar, eggs, flours and milk using electric beaters on low speed until combined, then beat on medium speed for 3 minutes, or until thick and creamy.
3. Pour the mixture into the prepared tin and smooth the surface.
4. Bake for 20–25 minutes, or lightly golden. Leave in the tin for 10 minutes, then turn out onto a wire rack to cool completely.
5. To make the icing, beat the cream cheese and icing sugar in a small bowl using electric beaters until light and creamy. Add the passionfruit pulp. Beat for 2 minutes, or until smooth and fluffy. Spoon over the cakes

classic cupcakes with icing

MAKES 12

250 g (9 oz/2 cups) self-raising flour

165 g (5 3/4 oz/3/4 cup) sugar

125 g (4 1/2 oz) unsalted butter, softened

3 eggs

3 tablespoons milk

1/2 teaspoon vanilla extract

caramel icing (frosting)

185 g (6 1/2 oz/1 1/2 cups) icing (confectioners') sugar

1 tablespoon milk

2 tablespoons golden syrup or honey

30 g (1 oz) unsalted butter, softened

1. Preheat the oven to 180°C (350°F/Gas 4). Line 18 standard muffin holes with paper patty cases.
2. Sift the flour and sugar into a bowl. Add the butter, eggs, milk and vanilla and beat until smooth. Fill the patty cases three-quarters full with the mixture.
3. Bake for 15 minutes, or until lightly golden. Cool on a wire rack.
4. To make the icing, put the icing sugar, milk, golden syrup and butter in a bowl and beat with a wooden spoon until smooth.
5. Spread over the cake with a flat-bladed knife.

honey and coconut cakes

MAKES 6

125 g (4 1/2 oz) unsalted butter, softened
140 g (4 1/2 oz/2/3 cup) raw sugar
2 large eggs, lightly beaten
1 teaspoon vanilla extract
90 g (3 1/4 oz/1/4 cup) honey
45 g (1 1/2 oz/1/2 cup) desiccated coconut
220 g (7 oz/1 3/4 cups) self-raising flour
1 teaspoon ground nutmeg
1/4 teaspoon ground cinnamon
1/4 teaspoon ground allspice
125 ml (4 fl oz/1/2 cup) milk

honey and cream cheese icing (frosting)

125 g (4 1/2 oz) cream cheese, softened
60 g (2 1/4 oz/1/2 cup) icing (confectioners') sugar
1 tablespoon honey

1. Preheat the oven to 180°C (350°F/ Gas 4). Lightly grease six 10 cm (4 inch) round cake tins and line the bases with baking paper.
2. Beat the butter and sugar in a bowl using electric beaters until creamy. Add the eggs gradually, beating well after each addition. Add the vanilla extract and honey. Beat until well combined.
3. Add the desiccated coconut. Using a metal spoon, fold in the sifted flour and spices and add the milk. Stir until just combined and the mixture is almost smooth. Spoon into the prepared tins and smooth the surface.
4. Bake for 30–35 minutes, or until lightly golden. Leave the cake in the tin for 10 minutes before turning out onto a wire rack to cool completely. Remove the baking paper from the cake.
5. To make the icing, beat the softened cream cheese in a bowl using electric beaters until creamy. Add the sifted icing sugar and honey, beating for 3 minutes or until the mixture is smooth and fluffy. Spread the icing over the whole cake using a flat-bladed knife.

Storage: These cakes can be stored for 4 days in an airtight container.

after dinner

apple pies

MAKES 4

125 g (4½ oz/1 cup) self-raising flour

125 g (4½ oz/1 cup) plain (all-purpose) flour

2 tablespoons custard powder (optional)

2 tablespoons caster (superfine) sugar

155 g (5½ oz) butter, chopped

1 egg, lightly beaten

filling

8 large apples (4 red and 4 green), peeled, cored and cut into pieces

4 thick strips lemon zest

1 cinnamon stick

8 whole cloves

90 g (3¼ oz/⅓ cup) caster (superfine) sugar

1. Sift the flours, custard powder and sugar into a bowl. Add the butter. Rub the butter into the flour mixture until the mixture resembles breadcrumbs.
2. Make a well in the centre. Stir in the egg and about 3–4 tablespoons of iced water and mix until the dough just comes together.
3. Turn onto a lightly floured surface and gently press together to form a ball. Wrap in plastic wrap and refrigerate for 20 minutes.
4. Combine the apples in a large saucepan with the zest, cinnamon stick, cloves, and 440 ml (15¼ fl oz/ 1¾ cups) of water and sugar. Cover and simmer gently for 10 minutes, or until the apples are tender. Remove from the heat and drain. Discard the zest, cinnamon and cloves. Allow to cool.
5. Preheat the oven to 180°C (350 F/Gas 4). Roll two-thirds of the dough between 2 sheets of baking paper. Line the base and sides of four 200 ml (7 fl oz) ovenproof bowls with the pastry. Refrigerate for 10 minutes.
6. Roll the rest of the pastry between 2 sheets of baking paper and cut to make lids for the pies. Spoon the apple mixture into the pie cases.
7. Brush the edges with a little beaten egg and milk. Lay the pastry over the top, pressing to seal the edges. Use a small knife to trim the pastry edges.
8. Use the remaining pastry scraps to decorate the top. Brush with the egg and milk. Make several slits in the pie top for steam holes. Bake for 45 minutes, or until golden and cooked through. Serve with custard, cream or ice cream.

berry gratin

SERVES 2

- 300 g (10½ oz) fresh mixed berries (raspberries, blueberries, strawberries)
- 4 egg yolks
- 2 tablespoons caster (superfine) sugar
- 3 tablespoons fresh orange juice
- ½ teaspoon finely grated orange zest

1. Lightly brush two shallow 315 ml (10¾ fl oz/1¼ cup) gratin or heatproof dishes with melted butter.
2. Arrange the mixed berries in the dish.
3. Put the egg yolks, sugar and the orange juice and zest in a small metal heatproof bowl and set over a saucepan of simmering water. Make sure the bowl does not touch the water.
4. Whisk the mixture using electric beaters for 4 minutes, or until thick and creamy.
5. Pour over the berries and place under a hot grill (broiler) for a few seconds, or until golden.

Variation: Any combination of fresh berries can be used in this gratin. Frozen berries can also be used if fresh berries are not available. Simply defrost and pat dry with paper towels before using.

baked peach puddings

MAKES 6

- 250 g (9 oz/2 cups) self-raising flour
- 125 g (4½ oz) butter
- 115 g (4 oz/½ cup) caster (superfine) sugar
- 100 g (3½ oz) marzipan
- 2 tablespoons citrus jam
- 2 tablespoons orange juice
- 150 g (5½ oz) dried peaches, chopped
- 125 ml (4 fl oz/½ cup) peach nectar
- 2 eggs, lightly beaten

peach sauce

- 440 g (15½ oz) tinned peach halves, with juice

1. Preheat the oven to 180°C (350°F/Gas 4). Brush six 175 ml (5½ fl oz/⅔ cup) ovenproof dishes with melted butter.
2. Sift the flour into a large mixing bowl. Combine the butter, sugar, marzipan, jam, orange juice, dried peaches and nectar in a saucepan. Stir over low heat until the butter and marzipan have melted and the sugar has dissolved. Remove from the heat.
3. Add the butter mixture and eggs to the flour. Using a wooden spoon, stir until well combined. Do not overmix. Spoon the mixture into the prepared dishes. Smooth the surface.
4. Bake for 25 minutes, or until a skewer comes out clean when inserted in the centre of the pudding. Serve warm with the peach sauce.
5. To make the peach sauce, place the peaches and juice in a food processor and blend for 20 seconds, or until the mixture is smooth. Transfer to a small saucepan. Stir over low heat for 2 minutes, or until the sauce is warmed through.

Note: Other dried fruits can be substituted for the peaches. And tinned fruit, such as dark pitted cherries, apricots or pears can be used in the sauce. It can also be served cold with vanilla ice cream.

baked vanilla custards

MAKES 4

oil, for greasing bowls
500 ml (17 fl oz/2 cups) milk
3 eggs
55 g (2 oz/1/4 cup) sugar
1/4 teaspoon vanilla extract
ground nutmeg, to sprinkle

1. Preheat the oven to 180°C (350°F/Gas 4). Brush four 200 ml (7 fl oz) ovenproof bowls with oil.
2. Whisk the milk, eggs, sugar and vanilla in a bowl for 2 minutes.
3. Pour the mixture into the bowls and sprinkle with the nutmeg.
4. Put the custard bowls into a larger roasting tin. Pour enough cold water into the tin to come halfway up the side of the bowls.
5. Bake for 20 minutes, then reduce the oven to 160°C (315°F/Gas 2–3). Bake for another 20 minutes, or until the custard is set. Take dishes out of water.
6. Serve the baked custard warm or cold, with fruit if you like.

peach galettes

MAKES 12

- 1 sheet ready-made puff pastry
- 600 g (1 lb 5 oz) peaches, pitted and thinly sliced
- 20 g (3/4 oz) butter, melted
- 1 tablespoon honey
- 1 tablespoon caster (superfine) sugar
- 1/4 teaspoon ground nutmeg
- 1 egg yolk
- 1 tablespoon milk
- 3 tablespoons apricot jam
- 25 g (1 oz/1/4 cup) flaked almonds, toasted

1. Lightly grease a baking tray. Cut out twelve 9.5 cm (3 3/4 inch) rounds from the pastry.
2. Combine the peach slices, butter, honey, sugar and nutmeg. Divide the peach mixture between the pastry rounds, leaving a 5 mm (1/4 inch) border around the edge.
3. Place on the tray and refrigerate for 30 minutes. Meanwhile, preheat the oven to 200°C (400°F/Gas 6).
4. Combine the egg yolk and milk. Brush over the edges of the pastry. Bake for 15 minutes, or until golden.
5. Combine the apricot jam and 1 tablespoon of water in a saucepan and stir over low heat until smooth. Brush the jam mixture over the hot galettes, then sprinkle with almonds. Allow to cool before serving.

apple puff squares

SERVES 4

- 1 sheet ready-rolled puff pastry
- 60 g (2 1/4 oz) butter, melted
- 2 tablespoons soft brown sugar
- 1/2 teaspoon ground mixed spice
- 2 granny smith apples, peeled, cored and cut into wedges

1. Preheat oven to 210°C (415°F/Gas 6–7). Lightly grease a baking tray.
2. Cut the pastry into 4 squares and place on the tray.
3. Combine the butter, sugar and spice and brush half the mixture over the pastry squares.
4. Cut the apple into very thin slices. Lay on top of the pastry squares, leaving a 1 cm (1/2 inch) border. Brush the squares with the rest of the butter mixture.
5. Bake for 15 minutes, or until golden.

baked cheesecake

SERVES 8–10

375 g (13 oz) plain sweet biscuits (cookies)
175 g (6 oz) unsalted butter, melted

filling

500 g (1 lb 2 oz) cream cheese
200 g (7 oz) caster (superfine) sugar
4 eggs
300 ml (10 1/2 fl oz) pouring (whipping) cream
2 tablespoons plain (all-purpose) flour
1 teaspoon ground cinnamon
1/4 teaspoon ground nutmeg
1 tablespoon lemon juice
2 teaspoons vanilla extract

1. Lightly grease a 23 cm (9 inch) round spring-form cake tin and line the base and side with baking paper.
2. Put the biscuits in a food processor and process into crumbs. Add the butter and process until well combined. Press firmly into the base and side of the tin. Refrigerate for 1 hour. Preheat the oven to 180°C (350°F/Gas 4).
3. To make the filling, beat the cream cheese and sugar together until creamy. Add the eggs and cream and beat for about 4 minute. Fold in the flour, cinnamon, nutmeg, lemon juice and vanilla.
4. Pour the filling into the chilled crust and smooth the surface. Bake for 1 hour, or until golden. Allow to cool to room temperature, then refrigerate until ready to serve.

warm strawberry and pecan tart

SERVES 6

125 g (4 1/2 oz) butter
55 g (2 oz/1/4 cup) caster (superfine) sugar
2 eggs, lightly beaten
1 tablespoon golden syrup or honey
40 g (1 1/2 oz) ground pecans
125 g (4 1/2 oz/1 cup) self-raising flour
250 g (9 oz) strawberries, hulled and sliced
80 g (2 3/4 oz/1/4 cup) plum jam
2–3 teaspoons apple juice

1. Preheat the oven to 180°C (350°F/Gas 4). Brush a 23 cm (9 inch) recess flan tin with melted butter. Coat the base and side evenly with flour. Shake off excess.
2. Beat the butter and sugar in a bowl using electric beaters until light and creamy. Add the eggs gradually, beating well after each addition. Add the syrup and beat until combined.
3. Transfer the mixture to a large bowl. Add the pecans. Fold in the sifted flour using a metal spoon. Stir until the mixture is just combined and almost smooth.
4. Spoon the mixture evenly into the prepared tin and smooth the surface.
5. Bake for 15 minutes or until a skewer comes out clean when inserted into the centre. Leave in the tin for 10 minutes, then turn onto a wire rack to cool.
6. Arrange the strawberry slices over the tart base.
7. Combine the jam and juice in a small saucepan. Stir over low heat until the jam has melted. Remove from the heat and brush over the warm tart. Serve with cream if you like.

mini berry pavlovas

MAKES 6

3 egg whites

230 g (8 oz/1 cup) caster (superfine) sugar

1 teaspoon icing (confectioners') sugar

50 g (1 3/4 oz) dark chocolate, melted

4 tablespoons pouring (whipping) cream

icing (confectioners') sugar, extra, to dust

1/2 teaspoon finely grated orange zest

assorted fresh fruit, to garnish, such as strawberries, cut into thin wedges, raspberries and blueberries, and passionfruit pulp

1. Preheat the oven to 150°C (300°F/Gas 2). Beat the egg whites in a large bowl until stiff peaks form. Add the icing sugar and beat until thick and very solid.
2. Draw twelve 7.5 cm (2 1/2 inch) circles onto two sheets of baking paper. Turn over and place onto a baking tray.
3. Spread the meringue mixture over each round. Spoon the remaining meringue into a piping (icing) bag.
4. Pipe three circles on top of each other, leaving a small hole in the centre.
5. Bake for 30 minutes, or until firm to touch. Leave to cool in the oven with the door slightly ajar.
6. Dip the bottom of the meringue bases into the melted chocolate, then place on trays covered with baking paper and allow to set.
7. Whisk the cream, extra icing sugar and orange zest until just thick. Spoon into the meringues. Top with berries and passionfruit pulp.

pear puffs

MAKES 36

dairy-free custard

4 egg yolks

90 g (3 1/4 oz/1/3 cup) sugar

2 1/2 tablespoons maize cornflour (cornstarch)

185 ml (6 fl oz/3/4 cup) pear juice

185 ml (6 fl oz/3/4 cup) rice drink

125 ml (4 fl oz/1/2 cup) canola oil

375 ml (13 oz/1 1/2 cups) cold water, plus a little extra

190 g (6 3/4 oz/1 1/4 cups) soy-free, gluten-free plain (all-purpose) flour

1/4 teaspoon bicarbonate of soda (baking soda)

1 teaspoon gluten-free baking powder

4 eggs

icing (confectioners') sugar, to dust

1. To make the custard, beat the egg yolks and sugar in a bowl using electric beaters until thick.
2. Blend the cornflour, pear juice and rice drink in a saucepan until smooth. Stir in the egg mixture and stir over low heat until thick. Pour into a bowl and cover with plastic wrap. Allow to cool.
3. Preheat the oven to 210°C (415°F/Gas 6–7). Cover two baking trays with baking paper.
4. Pour the oil and water into a saucepan and bring to the boil. Remove from the heat. Add the sifted dry ingredients, then return to the heat and stir until thick. Transfer to a bowl and allow to cool slightly.
5. Beat the mixture, adding the eggs one at a time and beating well between each addition until the mixture is thick and shiny.
6. Place level tablespoons of the mixture onto the prepared trays, then sprinkle or spray lightly all over with the extra cold water.
7. Bake for 10 minutes, or until starting to brown. Reduce the heat to 190°C (375°F/Gas 5) and bake for another 10–15 minutes, or until cooked through. Remove from the oven and allow to cool completely.
8. Split and fill with custard. Dust with icing sugar.

banana and plum crumble

SERVES 4–6

- 30 g (1 oz/1/4 cup) plain (all-purpose) flour
- 50 g (1 3/4 oz/1 cup) rolled oats
- 30 g (1 oz/1 cup) shredded coconut
- 45 g (1 1/2 oz/1/2 cup) soft brown sugar
- finely grated zest from 1 lime
- 100 g (3 1/2 oz) unsalted butter, cut into cubes
- 2 bananas, peeled and halved lengthways
- 6 plums, stoned, cut into quarters, then halved
- 3 tablespoons lime juice

1. Preheat the oven to 180°C (350°F/Gas 4).
2. Combine the flour, rolled oats, coconut, sugar and zest in a small bowl. Add the butter and, using your fingertips, rub the butter into the flour.
3. Divide the bananas and plums between four 250 ml (9 fl oz/1 cup) ramekins and pour over the lime juice. Toss to coat in the juice. Sprinkle the crumble mixture evenly over the fruit.
4. Bake for 20 minutes, or until the crumble is golden. Serve hot with ice cream or whipped cream.

caramel rice pudding

SERVES 4

110 g (3 3/4 oz/1/2 cup) short- or medium-grain rice

2 eggs

2 tablespoons soft brown sugar

375 ml (13 fl oz/1 1/2 cups) milk

2 tablespoons caramel topping

125 ml (4 fl oz/1/2 cup) pouring (whipping) cream

1/2 teaspoon freshly grated nutmeg, plus extra, to serve

1 Preheat the oven to 160°C (315°F/Gas 2–3). Grease a 1.5 litre (52 fl oz/6 cup) ovenproof dish.

2 Cook the rice in a saucepan of boiling water for 12 minutes, or until just tender. Drain, then cool slightly.

3 Put the eggs, sugar, milk, caramel topping and cream in a large bowl and whisk. Fold in the cooked rice.

4 Pour the rice mixture into the dish and sprinkle with the nutmeg. Put the dish in a baking tin and pour in enough boiling water to come halfway up the sides.

5 Bake for 30 minutes, then stir with a fork. Cook for a another 30 minutes, or until just set. Serve hot or warm. Sprinkle with the extra nutmeg before serving.

mango and passionfruit pies

MAKES 6

4 sheets ready-made puff pastry

3 ripe mangoes (900 g/2 lb), peeled and sliced or chopped, or 400 g (14 oz) tinned mango slices, drained

60 g (2¼ oz/¼ cup) passionfruit pulp, strained

1 tablespoon custard powder

90 g (3¼ oz/⅓ cup) caster (superfine) sugar

1 egg, lightly beaten

1. Preheat the oven to 190°C (375°F/Gas 5). Grease six 10 x 8 x 3 cm (4 x 3 x 1¼ inch) fluted flan tins or round pie dishes.
2. Cut out six 13 cm (5 inch) rounds from the pastry. Line the tins with the circles and trim the edges. Refrigerate until needed.
3. Combine the mango, passionfruit, custard powder and sugar in a bowl.
4. Cut out six 11 cm (4¼ inch) circles. Using any leftover pastry, cut shapes to decorate.
5. Fill the pastry cases with the mango mixture and brush the edges with egg.
6. Top with the pastry circles and press the edges to seal. Trim the edges. Decorate with the pastry shapes. Brush the tops with beaten egg.
7. Bake for 20–25 minutes, or until golden brown.

meringue-covered peaches

SERVES 2

2 peaches

20 g (3/4 oz) marzipan

2 egg whites

110 g (3 3/4 oz/1/2 cup) sugar

demerara sugar, to sprinkle

1. Preheat the oven to 220°C (425°F/Gas 7). Cut the peachs in half and remove the stones.
2. Place the peach halves in a bowl, cover with boiling water, and then cold water. Drain and peel the skin away.
3. Roll the marzipan into 4 balls and put in the gaps left by the stone. Place in a shallow, ovenproof dish.
4. Whisk the egg whites until soft peaks form. Gradually add the sugar and whisk to stiff peaks.
5. Cover the fruit with the mixture, using a fork to rough up the surface. Sprinkle with demerara sugar.
6. Bake for 5 minutes, or until lightly brown. Serve with cream or ice cream.

ricotta pots with raspberries

SERVES 4

4 eggs, separated

125 g (4 1/2 oz/1/2 cup) caster (superfine) sugar

350 g (11 1/4 oz) fresh ricotta cheese

35 g (1 1/4 oz/1/4 cup) finely chopped pistachio nuts

1 teaspoon grated lemon zest

2 tablespoons lemon juice

1 tablespoon vanilla sugar

200 g (7 oz) fresh raspberries

icing (confectioners') sugar, to dust

1. Preheat the oven to 180°C (350°F/Gas 4). Beat the egg yolks and sugar in a bowl until creamy. Add the ricotta, pistachio nuts, lemon zest and juice and mix.
2. Whisk the egg whites in a bowl until stiff peaks form. Beat in the vanilla sugar, then the ricotta mixture.
3. Grease four 250 ml (9 fl oz/1 cup) ramekins. Divide the raspberries among the dishes and spoon the ricotta filling over the top.
4. Place on a baking tray and bake for 20–25 minutes, or until puffed and lightly browned. Serve immediately, dusted with a little icing sugar.

peach and pineapple coconut crumble

MAKES 4

825 g (1 lb 13 oz) tinned peach halves
825 g (1 lb 13 oz) tinned pineapple pieces
2 tablespoons orange marmalade

topping

90 g ($3^1/_4$ oz) dried breadcrumbs
2 tablespoons plain (all-purpose) flour
20 g ($^3/_4$ oz/$^1/_3$ cup) shredded coconut
90 g ($3^1/_4$ oz) butter
1 tablespoon honey

1 Preheat the oven to 180°C (350°F/Gas 4). Drain the fruits, reserving 250 ml (9 fl oz/1 cup) of juice. Put the fruit in four 250 ml (9 fl oz/1 cup) shallow ovenproof dishes.

2 Combine the reserved juice and marmalade over low heat in a small saucepan. Bring to the boil, reduce the heat and simmer, uncovered, for about 5 minutes or until the mixture is a thick syrup. Pour over the fruit.

3 To make the topping, mix together the breadcrumbs, flour and coconut in a bowl.

4 Heat the butter and honey in a small saucepan until melted. Stir into the dry ingredients until combined. Spoon the mixture over fruit.

5 Bake for 15 minutes, or until the topping is golden. Serve warm with custard.

raspberry bread puddings

MAKES 4

50 g (1¾ oz) butter, softened

8–10 slices day-old white bread, crusts removed

300 g (10½ oz) frozen raspberries, thawed

3 eggs, lightly beaten

115 g (4 oz/½ cup) caster (superfine) sugar

310 ml (10¾ fl oz/1¼ cups) milk

icing (confectioners') sugar, to dust

1. Preheat the oven to 170°C (325°F/Gas 3). Brush four 200 ml (7 fl oz) ovenproof dishes with melted butter.
2. Butter the bread and slice in half diagonally. Arrange one-third of the bread, buttered side up, on the base of the prepared dishes. Cover with half the raspberries. Repeat layers, finishing with bread.
3. Whisk the eggs and sugar together. Add the milk and beat to combine. Stir in 2 tablespoons of water. Pour over the bread.
4. Put the dishes in a deep roasting tin. Pour hot water into the tin, to come halfway up the side of the dishes.
5. Bake for 30 minutes, or until the custard is set. Serve warm, dusted with icing sugar.

custard tarts

MAKES 12

250 g (9 oz/2 cups) plain (all-purpose) flour
60 g (2¼ oz/⅓ cup) rice flour
30 g (1 oz/¼ cup) icing (confectioners') sugar
120 g (4¼ oz) butter
1 egg yolk
3 tablespoons iced water
1 egg white, lightly beaten

filling

3 eggs
375 ml (13 fl oz/1½ cups) milk
55 g (2 oz/¼ cup) caster (superfine) sugar
1 teaspoon vanilla extract
½ teaspoon nutmeg or ground cinnamon

1 Place the flours, icing sugar and butter in food processor. Process for 20 seconds or until crumbly. Add the egg yolk and almost all the water. Process until mixture comes together. Turn onto a lightly floured surface and press together until smooth.

2 Divide into 12 portions, roll out and line twelve 10 cm (4 inch) fluted tart tins. Refrigerate for 20 minutes.

3 Preheat the oven to 180°C (350°F/Gas 4). Cover each pastry shell with baking paper and baking beads.

4 Place on a baking tray and bake for 10 minutes. Remove from the oven and discard the baking paper and baking beads. Bake for another 10 minutes, or until golden. Brush the base and sides beaten egg white.

5 To make the filling, reduce the oven to 150°C (300°F/Gas 2). Combine the eggs and milk in a bowl and whisk. Add the sugar and vanilla and whisk. Strain the mixture, then pour into the pastry cases. Sprinkle with nutmeg and bake for 50 minutes, or until just set. Serve at room temperature.

tiny strawberry tarts

MAKES 24

- 60 g (2¼ oz/½ cup) plain (all-purpose) flour
- 40 g (1½ oz) butter
- 1 tablespoon sugar
- 2 tablespoons custard powder
- 1 tablespoon sugar, extra
- 185 ml (6 fl oz/¾ cup) milk
- 12 small strawberries, halved
- 2 tablespoons baby apple gel, warmed

1. Sift the flour into a bowl. Rub the butter into the flour. Stir in the sugar. Add 1 tablespoon of water and mix. Turn onto a floured surface and knead until smooth. Cover and refrigerate for 30 minutes.
2. Preheat the oven to 180°C (350°F/Gas 4). Lightly grease 24 mini muffin holes.
3. Roll the pastry out to 2 mm (1/16 inch) thickness, and cut out circles using a 5 cm (2 inch) cutter. Press the circles into the holes. Bake for 15 minutes. Cool.
4. Mix the custard powder, sugar and milk in a saucepan and stir over low heat until thick.
5. Place a teaspoon of custard into each case. Top with half a strawberry and brush with warmed apple gel.

mini cherry galettes

MAKES 30

- 30 g (1 oz) unsalted butter
- 1½ tablespoons caster (superfine) sugar
- 1 egg yolk
- ½ teaspoon vanilla extract
- 95 g (3¼ oz/½ cup) ground almonds
- 1 tablespoon plain (all-purpose) flour
- 2 sheets ready-rolled puff pastry, thawed
- 670 g (1 lb 8 oz) jar pitted morello cherries, well drained
- 160 g (5¾ oz/½ cup) cherry jam

1. Preheat the oven to 180°C (350°F/Gas 4). Line a baking tray with baking paper.
2. Beat the butter and sugar until creamy. Mix in the egg yolk, vanilla, almonds and flour. Chill.
3. Cut 30 circles from the pastry using a 5 cm (2 inch) round cutter. Place half the circles on the tray and prick with a fork. Cover with baking paper and weigh down with a baking tray.
4. Bake for 10 minutes. Repeat with remaining circles.
5. Place 1 teaspoon of almond mixture in the centre of each circle. Press a cherry onto the almond mixture.
6. Bake for 10 minutes, or until lightly browned. Brush the cherries with the warmed jam.

individual apple charlottes with jam sauce

SERVES 4

5 cooking apples, peeled, cored, thinly sliced

2 tablespoons soft brown sugar

1/4 teaspoon ground cinnamon

2 loaves day-old white bread, crusts removed

150 g (5 1/2 oz) unsalted butter, melted

jam sauce

315 g (11 oz/1 cup) raspberry jam

1 teaspoon grated lemon zest

115 g (4 oz/1/2 cup) caster (superfine) sugar

1 Preheat the oven to 180°C (350°F/Gas 4). Grease six 250 ml (9 fl oz/1 cup) capacity ovenproof dishes.

2 Put the apple slices in a saucepan with the sugar, cinnamon and enough water to cover. Cook until tender and drain well. Cool.

3 Using a biscuit cutter, cut 8 rounds from the bread slices to fit the tops and bases of the dishes.

4 Cut the remaining slices into fingers 2 cm (3/4 inch) wide. Trim to fit the height of the dish.

5 Dip 4 rounds into melted butter. Press into the base of the dishes. Line the sides with the bread fingers.

6 Fill each dish with the cooked apple and top with a round of bread, dipped in butter. Press down to seal.

7 Put the dishes on a baking tray. Bake for 20 minutes. Turn out onto plates. Serve with the jam sauce.

8 To make the jam sauce, combine the ingredients in a saucepan. Add 125 ml (4 fl oz/1/2 cup) of water. Bring to the boil and simmer for 20 minutes. Serve warm.

queen of puddings

SERVES 6

80 g (2¾ oz/1 cup) fresh white breadcrumbs
500 ml (17 fl oz/2 cups) milk, scalded
2 eggs yolks
55 g (2 oz/¼ cup) sugar
3 tablespoons strawberry jam
150 g (5½ oz) strawberries, sliced

meringue

110 g (3¾ oz/½ cup) caster (superfine) sugar
4 egg whites

1 Preheat the oven to 180°C (350°F/Gas 4). Put the breadcrumbs in a bowl with the hot milk and leave for 10 minutes.

2 Beat the egg yolks with half the sugar and stir into the crumb mixture.

3 Spoon the mixture into a greased 900 ml (30 fl oz) ovenproof bowl and bake for 45 minutes, or until firm. Reduce the oven to warm 160°C (315°F/Gas 2–3).

4 Combine the jam and sliced strawberries and spread over the pudding.

5 To make the meringue, whisk the egg whites until stiff, then beat in the sugar. Swirl over the top of the pudding.

6 Bake for 8–10 minutes, or until the meringue is set and lightly browned. Serve hot or warm.

fresh fruit tarts

MAKES 36

750 g (1 lb 10 oz) ready-made sweet shortcrust pastry

kiwi fruit tarts

250 g (9 oz) cream cheese, at room temperature

4 tablespoons icing (confectioners') sugar

1 teaspoon grated lemon zest

1 teaspoon lemon juice

1–2 kiwi fruit, sliced, to serve

110 g (3¾ oz) apple baby gel

blueberry tarts

2 tablespoons cornflour (cornstarch)

1 teaspoon grated lemon zest

2 tablespoons lemon juice

2 tablespoons caster (superfine) sugar

185 ml (6 fl oz/¾ cup) milk

1 egg, lightly beaten

3 tablespoons pouring (whipping) cream

250 g (9 oz) fresh blueberries

icing (confectioners') sugar, to dust

1 Roll out the pastry and cut out 12 rounds using a 7 cm (2¾ inch) cutter. Line deep patty pans with the pastry rounds. Refrigerate for 10 minutes.

2 Cover each pastry shell with baking paper and fill with baking beads. Bake for 10 minutes. Remove from the oven and remove the baking paper and beads. Bake the pastry for a further 5–7 minutes, or until lightly golden. Cool before filling.

3 To make the kiwi fruit tarts, beat the cream cheese, icing sugar, lemon zest and juice using electric beaters. Spoon into the pastry cases. Arrange slices of kiwi fruit over the cream. Gently heat the apple gel until melted, then brush over the fruit.

4 To make the blueberry tarts, combine the cornflour, lemon zest, juice, caster sugar, milk and egg in a saucepan. Stir over low heat until the mixture boils and thickens, then cook for 1 minute. Cover and cool to room temperature, then whisk in the cream. Spoon into the pastry cases and cover with the blueberries. Sprinkle with icing sugar.

chocolate roll

SERVES 6–8

3 eggs

125 g (4½ oz/½ cup) caster (superfine) sugar

30 g (1 oz/¼ cup) plain (all-purpose) flour

2 tablespoons cocoa powder

250 ml (9 fl oz/1 cup) pouring (whipping) cream

1 tablespoon icing (confectioners') sugar

½ teaspoon vanilla extract

icing (confectioners') sugar, extra, to dust

1. Preheat the oven to 200°C (400°F/Gas 6). Grease a 25 x 30 cm (10 x 12 inch) Swiss roll tin (jelly roll tin). Line with paper and grease the paper.
2. Beat the eggs and 90 g (3 oz/⅓ cup) of the caster sugar in a bowl using electric beaters until thick.
3. Sift the flour and cocoa together and fold into the egg mixture. Spread into the tin. Bake for 12 minutes.
4. Place a tea towel on a work surface, cover with baking paper and sprinkle with the caster sugar. Turn the cake out onto the paper. Trim the edges.
5. Roll the cake up from the long side, rolling the paper inside the roll. Leave on a wire rack for 5 minutes, then unroll and cool.
6. Beat the cream, icing sugar and vanilla until stiff peaks form. Spread over the cake.
7. Roll the cake up again. Place the cake, seam-side-down, on a tray. Refrigerate for 30 minutes. Dust with icing sugar, then cut into slices to serve.

party time

alphabet cookies

MAKES ABOUT 20

vanilla cookies

125 g (4½ oz) unsalted butter, softened

125 g (4½ oz) caster (superfine) sugar

30 ml (1 fl oz) milk

1 teaspoon vanilla extract

185 g (6½ oz/1½ cups) self-raising flour

60 g (2¼ oz/½ cup) custard powder

icing (frosting)

60 g (2¼ oz/½ cup) icing (confectioners') sugar, sifted

5 g (⅛ oz) butter

1 tablespoons hot water

¼ teaspoon vanilla extract

few drops of various food colouring (optional)

1 Preheat the oven to 190°C (375°F/Gas 5). Line two trays with baking paper.

2 Beat the butter and caster sugar in a bowl using electric beaters for 3–5 minutes, or until fluffy.

3 Add the milk and vanilla extract and beat until combined. Add the self-raising flour and custard powder and use a knife to mix to a soft dough.

4 Turn onto a floured surface and knead for 1 minute, or until smooth. Roll out the dough between two sheets of baking paper, to 5 mm (¼ inch) thick.

5 Cut the dough into shapes using alphabet cutters. Press the remaining dough together and re-roll. Cut out shapes and place the biscuits on the trays.

6 Bake for 15–18 minutes, until golden. Cool on the trays for 3 minutes, then transfer to a wire rack to cool.

7 To make the icing, blend all the ingredients together until smooth. If using various colours, separate into bowls, then add colouring. Spread over the biscuits.

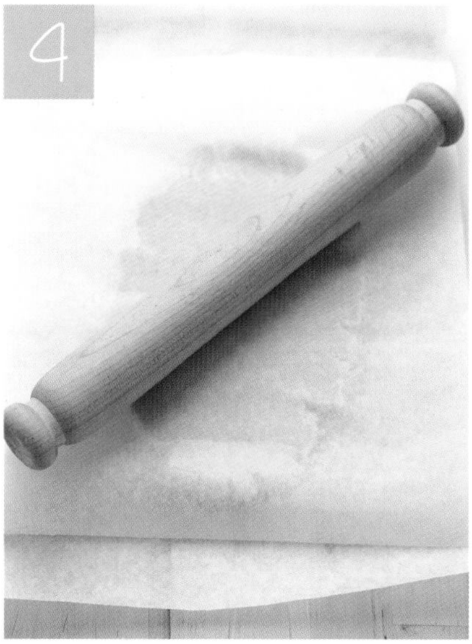

pretty party stars

MAKES 60

125 g (4½ oz) unsalted butter, softened

55 g (2 oz/¼ cup) caster (superfine) sugar

1 egg, lightly beaten

2 tablespoons honey

2 tablespoons grated lemon zest

310 g (11 oz/2½ cups) plain (all-purpose) flour

½ teaspoon ground ginger

icing (frosting)

215 g (7½ oz/1¾ cups) icing (confectioners') sugar, sifted

2–3 tablespoons lemon juice

coloured cachous, to decorate

1. Preheat oven to 180°C (350°F/Gas 4). Line 2 baking trays with baking paper. Lightly grease the paper.
2. Beat the butter and sugar in a mixing bowl until light and creamy. Beat in the egg. Beat in the honey and lemon zest.
3. Using a metal spoon, fold in the combined sifted flour and ginger. Shape the dough into a ball. Cover with plastic wrap and refrigerate for 15 minutes.
4. Roll the pastry between two sheets of plastic wrap to a 5 mm (¼ inch) thickness. Cut into stars with a 5 cm (2 inch) cutter. Place the pastry shapes onto the prepared trays.
5. Bake for 10 minutes, or until lightly golden. Leave the biscuits on trays for 5 minutes, then turn out onto a wire rack to cool.
6. To make the icing, combine the sifted icing sugar and some of the lemon juice. Spread the icing over the stars using a knife. Decorate with the cachous.

Note: Store in an airtight container between sheets of greaseproof paper in a cool, dry place for up to 7 days.

stained-glass window biscuits

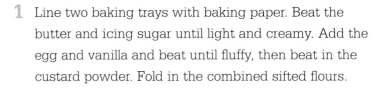

MAKES ABOUT 16

150 g (5 1/2 oz) unsalted butter, cubed, softened

60 g (2 1/4 oz/1/2 cup) icing (confectioners') sugar

1 egg

1 teaspoon vanilla extract

40 g (1 1/2 oz/1/3 cup) custard powder

250 g (9 oz/2 cups) plain (all-purpose) flour

30 g (1 oz/1/4 cup) self-raising flour

150 g (5 1/2 oz) assorted boiled lollies

1 beaten egg, to glaze

1. Line two baking trays with baking paper. Beat the butter and icing sugar until light and creamy. Add the egg and vanilla and beat until fluffy, then beat in the custard powder. Fold in the combined sifted flours.
2. Turn onto a lightly floured surface and knead until smooth. Roll between 2 sheets of baking paper to 3 mm (1/8 inch) thick. Refrigerate for 15 minutes, or until firm.
3. Preheat the oven to 200°C (400°F/Gas 6). Separate the lollies into their different colours and crush using a rolling pin.
4. Cut out the dough with a 9.5 cm (3 1/2 inch) fluted round cutter. Lay on the trays. Use small cutters to cut shapes from inside the circles.
5. Glaze the biscuits with the beaten egg and bake for 5 minutes. Don't let the glaze drip into the cutout sections of the biscuits or the stained glass will be cloudy.
6. Fill each cut-out section with a different-coloured lolly. Bake for 5–6 minutes, or until the lollies melt. Leave for 10 minutes, then cool on a wire rack.

marble cake

SERVES 8–10

25 g (1 oz) unsalted butter

115 g (4 oz/1/2 cup) caster (superfine) sugar

2 eggs

1/2 teaspoon vanilla extract

250 g (9 oz/2 cups) self-raising flour, sifted

125 ml (4 fl oz/1/2 cup) milk

2 tablespoons unsweetened cocoa

1/8 teaspoon bicarbonate of soda (baking soda)

1 tablespoon milk, extra

few drops pink food colouring

icing (frosting)

125 g (41/2 oz/1 cup) icing (confectioners') sugar, sifted

15 g (1/2 oz) unsalted butter, softened

1/2 teaspoon vanilla extract

few drops red food colouring, extra

1. Preheat the oven to 180°C (350°F/Gas 4). Grease and flour a 9 x 23 cm (31/2 x 9 inch) loaf (bar) tin.
2. Cream the butter and sugar together until light and fluffy. Add the eggs one at a time, beating well. Mix in vanilla. Fold in flour alternately with milk.
3. Divide the mixture into 3 separate bowls. Add the cocoa, soda and milk to one. Leave one plain. Stir food colouring into the remaining bowl.
4. Drop alternate colours into the tin.
5. Draw a skewer or knife through the mixture in circles to streak the colours. Bake for 40–45 minutes, or until a skewer poked in the middle comes out clean.
6. Cool in the tin for 5 minutes, then turn out onto a wire rack to cool completely.
7. To make the icing, beat the ingredients and add 1–2 tablespoons of water. Spread over the top of cake.

polka dot cookies

MAKES ABOUT 50

- 125 g (4 1/2 oz) unsalted butter, cubed
- 125 g (4 1/2 oz/1/2 cup) caster (superfine) sugar
- 1 egg
- 1/4 teaspoon vanilla extract
- 125 g (4 1/2 oz/1 cup) plain (all-purpose) flour
- 125 g (4 1/2 oz/1 cup) self-raising flour
- 1 cup smarties

1. Preheat the oven to 160°C (315°F/Gas 2–3). Line a baking tray with baking paper.
2. Beat the butter and caster sugar using electric beaters until light and fluffy. Add the egg and vanilla extract and beat well.
3. Sift the flours and fold in to form a soft dough.
4. Turn out onto a sheet of baking paper, cover with another sheet and roll out to 5 mm (1/4 inch) thick.
5. Using biscuit cutters, cut out circles and place on the tray. Press the smarties into the biscuits.
6. Bake in batches for 10–15 minutes, or until golden. Cool on a wire rack.

jelly dipped cupcakes

MAKES 30

250 g (9 oz/2 cups) self-raising flour

165 g (5¾ oz/¾ cup) sugar

125 g (4½ oz) unsalted butter, softened

3 eggs

3 tablespoons milk

½ teaspoon vanilla extract

icing (frosting)

125 g (4½ oz/1 cup) icing (confectioners') sugar

red and green food colouring

jelly

85 g (3 oz) packet of red jelly crystals

85 g (3 oz) packet green jelly crystals

400 ml (14 fl oz) boiling water

180 g (6 oz/2 cups) desiccated coconut, to coat

1. Preheat the oven to 180°C (350°F/Gas 4). Line 18 standard muffin holes with paper patty cases.
2. Sift the flour and sugar into a bowl. Add the butter, eggs, milk and vanilla and beat until smooth. Fill the patty cases three-quarters full with the mixture.
3. Bake for 15 minutes, or until golden. Remove from the muffin holes and place onto a wire rack to cool.
4. To make the icing, mix the icing sugar and 1–2 tablespoons of water, until thick. Divide among separate bowls and add red food colouring to one bowl and green to the other.
5. Put jelly crystals into separate bowls. Pour half of the boiling water into each bowl and stir to dissolve. Allow to cool, but not to set.
6. Dip each cake into either green or red jelly. Roll the cakes in the coconut. Refrigerate overnight to set. Serve chilled.

traffic light biscuits

MAKES 15

125 g (4 1/2 oz) unsalted butter, cubed and softened

125 g (4 1/2 oz/1/2 cup) caster (superfine) sugar

1/2 teaspoon vanilla extract

185 g (6 1/2 oz/1 1/2 cups) plain (all-purpose) flour

60 g (2 1/4 oz/1/2 cup) custard powder

30 ml (1 fl oz) milk

1 tablespoon strawberry jam

2 tablespoons apricot jam

green food colouring

1. Preheat the oven to 200°C (400°F/Gas 6). Line a baking tray with baking paper.
2. Beat the butter and caster sugar until light and creamy. Add the vanilla and beat until combined.
3. Sift the flour and custard powder into the butter mixture. Add the milk and using a flat-bladed or palette knife, mix the ingredients together to form a soft dough. Turn out onto a lightly floured surface.
4. Roll the dough out to a neat rectangle 21 x 40 cm (8 1/2 x 16 inches). Using a ruler as a guide, cut out 30 rectangles, each measuring 4 x 8 cm (1 1/4 x 3 1/4 inches).
5. Stir the strawberry jam in a bowl until smooth. Divide the apricot jam into 2 bowls and add a few drops of green food colouring to one of the bowls. Stir both until smooth. Put a small amount of red, yellow and green jam (to resemble traffic lights) on 15 of the rectangles. Spread the jam out a little.
6. Using a plain cutter with a 2 cm (3/4 inch) hole, cut 3 evenly spaced holes from the other 15 rectangles. Take a biscuit with the holes and sandwich on top of one of the biscuits with the jam. Press gently but firmly to show the jam coming through the holes. Repeat with the remaining rectangles and jam.
7. Place the biscuits onto the tray and bake for 15–20 minutes, or until lightly golden. Leave on the tray for 5 minutes, then cool on a wire rack.

custard rolls

MAKES 18

375 ml (13 fl oz/1½ cups) milk
115 g (4 oz/½ cup) caster (superfine) sugar
60 g (2¼ oz/½ cup) semolina
1 teaspoon grated lemon zest
1 egg, lightly beaten
12 sheets filo pastry
125 g (4½ oz) unsalted butter, melted
2 tablespoons icing (confectioners') sugar
½ teaspoon ground cinnamon

1. Put the milk, caster sugar, semolina and lemon zest in a saucepan and bring to the boil, stirring. Reduce the heat and simmer for 3 minutes.
2. Remove from the heat and whisk in the egg. Pour the custard into a bowl, cover the surface with plastic wrap and set aside to cool.
3. Preheat the oven to 180°C (350°F/Gas 4). Lightly brush two baking trays with melted butter.
4. Brush one pastry sheet with melted butter, then top with another. Cut lengthways into three strips. Brush the edges with melted butter.
5. Spoon 1 tablespoon of the custard 5 cm (2 inches) in from the short edge of each pastry strip.
6. Roll the pastry over the filling. Fold the ends in, then roll up. Repeat with the remaining pastry and custard.
7. Arrange on the trays and brush with butter. Bake for 12–15 minutes, or until golden. Cool on a wire rack. Dust with the combined icing sugar and cinnamon.

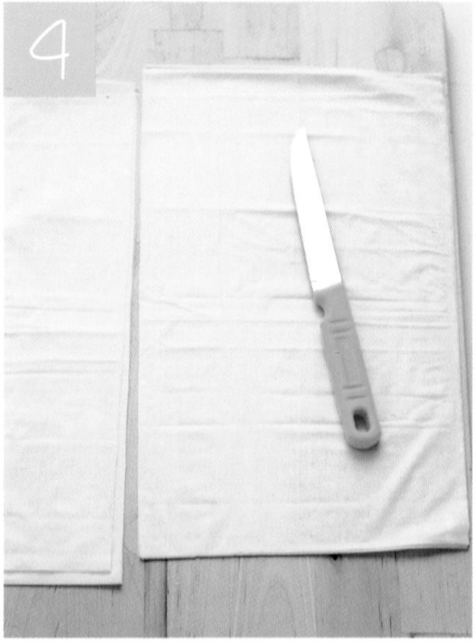

caramel centres

MAKES 36

300 g ($10\frac{1}{2}$ oz) unsalted butter

125 g ($4\frac{1}{2}$ oz/$\frac{1}{2}$ cup) caster (superfine) sugar

2 teaspoons vanilla extract

185 g ($6\frac{1}{2}$ oz/$1\frac{1}{2}$ cups) plain (all-purpose) flour

85 g (3 oz/$\frac{2}{3}$ cup) self-raising flour

caramel topping

50 g ($1\frac{3}{4}$ oz) unsalted butter, cubed and softened

2 tablespoons soft brown sugar

1 tablespoon golden syrup

125 ml (4 fl oz/$\frac{1}{2}$ cup) condensed milk

100 g ($3\frac{1}{2}$ oz) chocolate, melted

1. Preheat the oven to 180°C (350°F/Gas 4). Line 2 baking trays with baking paper.
2. Beat the butter and sugar until creamy and add the vanilla. Stir in the combined sifted flours and mix to a smooth dough.
3. Roll 3 teaspoons of the mixture into balls and place on the trays. Using your thumb, make a deep indentation in the centre of each biscuit. Bake for 10–15 minutes, or until lightly golden. Leave for 5 minutes, then cool on a wire rack.
4. To make the caramel topping, place the butter, sugar and syrup in a heavy-based pan. Stir over low heat until the sugar dissolves. Add the condensed milk and stir for about 5–10 minutes, or until golden.
5. Fill the cavity of each biscuit with the caramel and cool. When the caramel is cold, flatten with a wet finger.
6. Spread the chocolate on top.

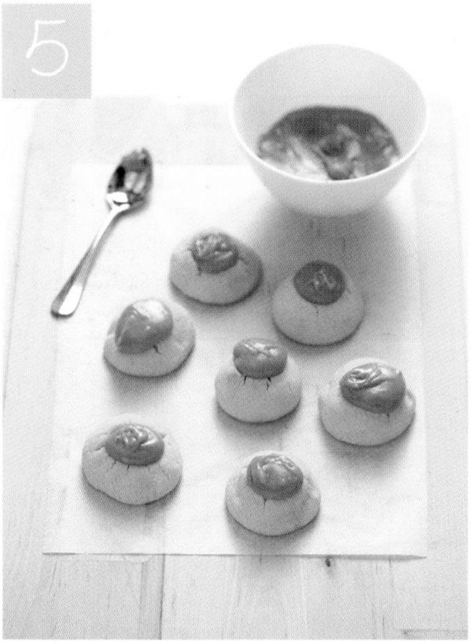

choc mint cone cakes

MAKES 24

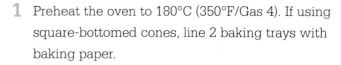

- 340 g (11¾ oz) packet chocolate cake mix
- 24 small waffle cones or square-bottomed ice cream cones
- 24 after-dinner mints
- 24 assorted lollies
- sprinkles, to decorate

1. Preheat the oven to 180°C (350°F/Gas 4). If using square-bottomed cones, line 2 baking trays with baking paper.
2. Prepare the cake mix following the directions on the packet.
3. Spoon 1½ tablespoons of the cake mixture into each ice cream cone. Wedge the waffle cones into a wide oven rack. If using square-bottomed cones, place on the prepared baking trays.
4. Bake for 20 minutes, or until the cakes are firm when pressed with the back of a spoon. Remove from the oven.
5. When cool, put an after-dinner mint on top of each cone cake. Put the cones in a warm oven for about 1–2 minutes to melt mint slightly. Place a lolly on the mint and decorate with sprinkles.

two-tone fudge brownies

MAKES 20

125 g ($4^1/_2$ oz) unsalted butter
90 g ($3^1/_4$ oz) chopped milk chocolate
250 g (9 oz) sugar
2 teaspoons vanilla extract
2 eggs
120 g ($4^1/_4$ oz) sifted plain (all-purpose) flour
90 g ($3^1/_4$ oz) white chocolate buttons

1 Preheat the oven to 180°C (350°F/Gas 4). Grease a 20 cm (8 inch) square cake tin.

2 Stir 60 g ($2^1/_4$ oz) of the butter and the chopped milk chocolate in a heatproof bowl set over a saucepan of simmering water until just melted.

3 Beat 125 g ($4^1/_2$ oz) sugar, 1 teaspoon vanilla extract and 1 egg in a bowl and stir in the chocolate mixture. Stir in 60 g ($2^1/_4$ oz) of the plain flour until combined, then set aside.

4 Stir 60 g ($2^1/_4$ oz) of the butter and the white chocolate buttons in a heatproof bowl set over a saucepan of simmering water until just melted.

5 Beat 125 g ($4^1/_2$ oz) sugar, 1 teaspoon vanilla extract and 1 egg in a bowl and stir in the white chocolate mixture. Stir in 60 g ($2^1/_4$ oz) of the plain flour until combined, then set aside.

6 Drop large spoonfuls of the two mixtures into the tin, without mixing them together. Gently smooth the surface and bake for 35 minutes, or until firm. Cool in the tin before cutting.

clock cake

SERVES 8

20 cm (8 inch) ready-made sponge cake

butter cream

125 g (4 1/2 oz) unsalted butter

1 1/2 cups icing (confectioners') sugar

500 g (1 lb 2 oz) white sugarpaste icing

pink food colouring

blue food colouring

smarties

2 different coloured jelly snakes

1. To make the butter cream, beat the butter and sugar in a bowl using electric beaters until thick and smooth.
2. Tint the butter cream to a bright blue and cover the cake using a flat-bladed knife or a spatula.
3. Arrange the smarties around the side.
4. To make the numbers, add the pink food colouring to the icing. Roll out to a 5 mm (1/4 inch) thickness and cut out numbers..
5. Cut the jelly snakes to make the hands of the clock, pointing them to the child's age. Put a smartie in the centre of the cake.

ice cream brownie sandwiches

SERVES 6

1 litre (35 fl oz/4 cups) vanilla ice cream, slightly softened

125 g (4½ oz) unsalted butter, chopped

185 g (6½ oz) dark chocolate, chopped

250 g (9 oz/1 cup) caster (superfine) sugar

2 eggs, lightly beaten

125 g (4½ oz/1 cup) plain (all-purpose) flour, sifted

60 g (2¼ oz/½ cup) chopped walnuts or hazelnuts

unsweetened cocoa, to dust

1. Preheat the oven to 180°C (350°F/Gas 4). Line a baking tray with baking paper.
2. Spread out the ice cream to form a 15 x 20 cm (6 x 8 inch) rectangle. Cover the surface with baking paper and re-freeze it.
3. Lightly grease a 20 x 30 cm (8 x 12 inch) baking tin and line the base with baking paper, leaving a little hanging over the two longer sides.
4. Put the butter and chocolate in a heatproof bowl and set over a saucepan of simmering water. Stir the chocolate until melted. Remove and cool slightly.
5. Whisk in the sugar and eggs, then add the flour and walnuts. Stir well, then spoon into the tin.
6. Bake for 40 minutes, or until firm. Cool in the tin.
7. Cut the brownie into 12 portions and the ice cream into six.
8. Sandwich the ice cream between two pieces of brownie and dust with cocoa.

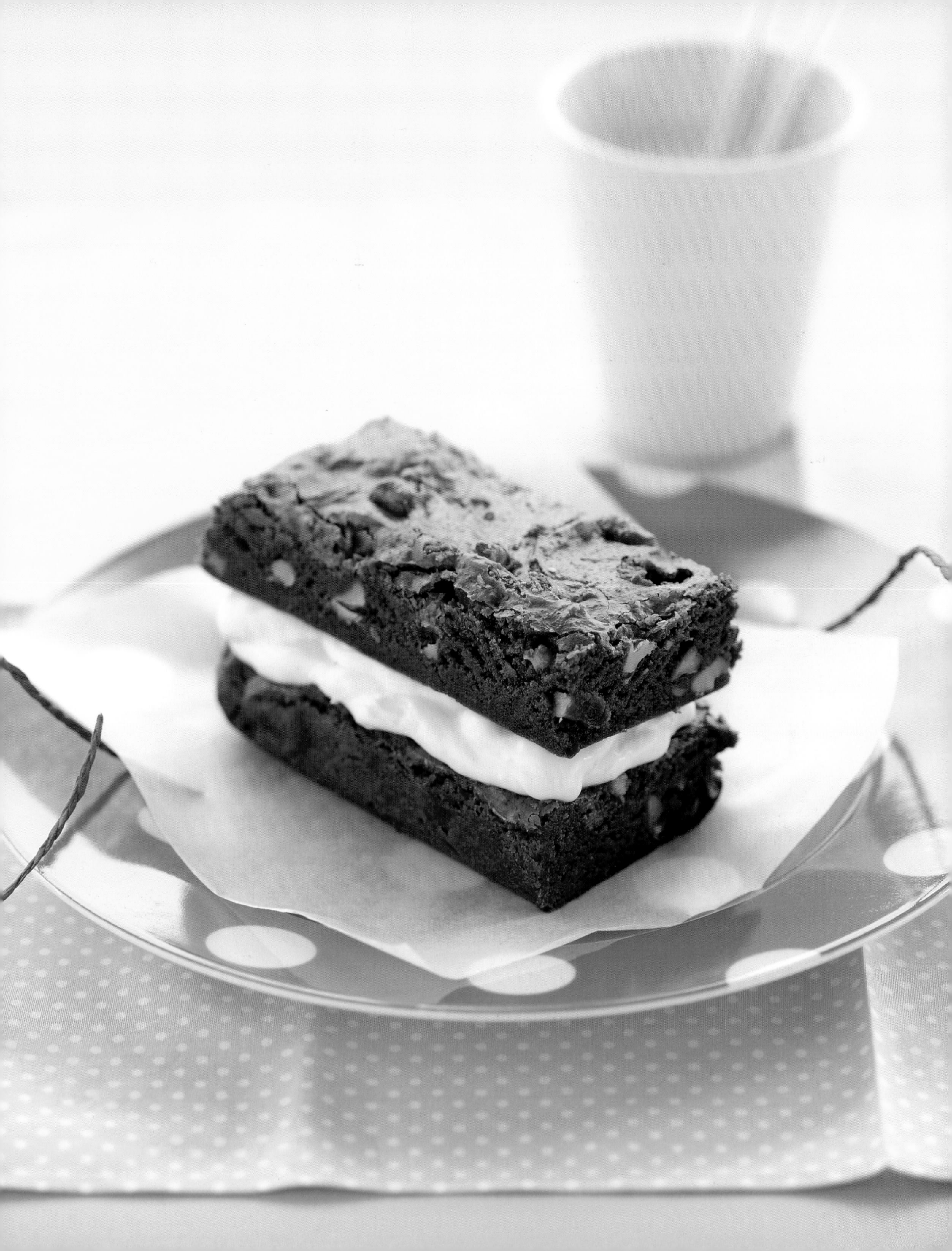

chocolate teddy biscuits

MAKES ABOUT 15

45 g (1 1/2 oz) chocolate, roughly chopped
125 g (4 1/2 oz) unsalted butter, chopped
30 g (1 oz/1/4 cup) icing (confectioners') sugar
1 egg, lightly beaten
1 tablespoon cornflour (cornstarch)
185 g (6 1/2 oz/1 1/2 cups) plain (all-purpose) flour
2 tablespoons unsweetened cocoa powder
50 g (1 3/4 oz) white chocolate melts
30 brown smarties, for eyes
15 white jellybeans, for nose
red sour straps, for bowties

1. Preheat oven to 180°C (350°F/Gas 4). Grease 2 baking trays and line with baking paper.
2. Put the chocolate in a heatproof bowl and set over a small saucepan of simmering water. Stir the chocolate until melted and smooth.
3. Beat the butter and sugar in a bowl using electric beaters until light and fluffy. Add the egg and melted chocolate and beat well.
4. Sift the cornflour, plain flour and cocoa into the bowl with the chocolate mixture and mix well with a flat bladed knife.
5. Knead the dough on a lightly floured surface for about 30 seconds, or until smooth.
6. Roll the dough out to a 1 cm (1/2 inch) thickness. Use a teddy bear head cookie cutter to cut out shapes in the dough. Put the biscuits on the trays
7. Bake for 20 minutes, or until firm to touch.
8. Put the white chocolate melts in a heatproof bowl and setl over a saucepan of simmering water. Stir until the chocolate has melted.
9. Decorate the biscuits with lollies by sticking them on with melted white chocolate.

crackle cookies

MAKES ABOUT 60

125 g (4 1/2 oz) unsalted butter, cubed and softened
370 g (13 oz/2 cups) soft brown sugar
1 teaspoon vanilla extract
2 eggs
60 g (2 1/4 oz) dark chocolate, melted
4 tablespoons milk
340 g (11 3/4 oz/2 3/4 cups) plain (all-purpose) flour
2 tablespoons unsweetened cocoa powder
2 teaspoons baking powder
1/4 teaspoon ground allspice
85 g (3 oz/2/3 cup) chopped pecan nuts
icing (confectioners') sugar, to coat

1. Lightly grease 2 baking trays. Beat the butter, sugar and vanilla until light and creamy. Beat in the eggs, one at a time. Stir the chocolate and milk into the butter mixture.
2. Sift the flour, cocoa, baking powder, allspice and a pinch of salt into the butter mixture and mix well. Stir the pecans through. Refrigerate for at least 3 hours, or overnight.
3. Preheat the oven to 180°C (350°F/Gas 4). Roll tablespoons of the mixture into balls and roll each in the icing sugar to coat.
4. Place well apart on the trays. Bake for 20–25 minutes, or until lightly browned. Leave for 3–4 minutes, then cool on a wire rack.

cat and mouse cakes

MAKES 12

125 g (4 1/2 oz) butter

1 teaspoon finely grated orange zest

170 g (6 oz/3/4 cup caster (superfine) sugar

2 eggs, lightly beaten

250 g (9 oz/2 cups) self-raising flour

125 ml (4 fl oz/1/2 cup) milk

icing (frosting)

125 g (4 1/2 oz) unsalted butter

250 g (9 oz/2 cups) icing (confectioners') sugar

2 tablespoons milk

food colouring

assorted sweets, such as sour fruit straps, marshmallow hearts, jelly beans, after-dinner mints and licorice all-sorts, to decorate

1 Preheat the oven to 180°C (350°F/Gas 4). Grease twelve 125 ml (4 fl oz/1/2 cup) muffin holes.

2 Beat the butter, zest and sugar in a bowl using electric beaters until light and creamy. Add the eggs gradually, beating well after each addition.

3 Using a large metal spoon, fold in the sifted flour alternately with the milk. Stir until mixture is smooth.

4 Spoon into the prepared muffin holes, filling two-thirds of each hole.

5 Bake for 20 minutes, or until lightly golden. Turn onto a wire rack to cool.

6 Spread the top of each cake with frosting and decorate with sweets to make faces.

7 To make the icing, using electric beaters, beat the butter in a small mixing bowl until light and fluffy. Add the sifted icing sugar and milk and beat until mixture is smooth. Tint portions of the icing in different colours.

angel food cake with chocolate sauce

SERVES 8

125 g (4 1/2 oz/1 cup) plain (all-purpose) flour

250 g (9 oz/1 cup) caster (superfine) sugar

10 egg whites, at room temperature

1 teaspoon cream of tartar

1/2 teaspoon vanilla extract

chocolate sauce

250 g (9 oz) dark chocolate, chopped

185 ml (6 fl oz/3/4 cup) pouring (whipping) cream

50 g (1 3/4 oz) unsalted butter, chopped

silver cachous (balls), to decorate

1 Preheat the oven to 180°C (350°F/Gas 4). Have an ungreased angel cake tin ready.

2 Sift the flour and 125 g (4 1/2 oz/1/2 cup) of the sugar four times into a large bowl. Set aside.

3 Beat the egg whites, cream of tartar and 1/4 teaspoon salt in a bowl using electric beaters until soft peaks form. Gradually add the remaining sugar and beat until thick and glossy.

4 Add the vanilla extract. Sift half the flour and sugar mixture over the meringue and gently fold into the mixture with a metal spoon. Repeat with the remaining flour and sugar. Spoon into the cake tin.

5 Bake for 45 minutes, or until a skewer comes out clean when inserted into the centre of the cake. Gently loosen around the side of the cake with a spatula, then turn the cake out onto a wire rack to cool completely.

6 To make the sauce, put the chocolate, cream and butter in a saucepan. Stir over low heat until the chocolate has melted and the mixture is smooth. Drizzle over the cake and sprinkle with cachous.

Note: Ensure the tin is very clean and not greased or the cake will not rise and will slip down the side of the tin.

chocolate coconut frosties

MAKES ABOUT 20

125 g (4 1/2 oz) unsalted butter, cubed and softened

125 g (4 1/2 oz/1 cup) icing (confectioners') sugar, sifted

1 egg

155 g (5 1/2 oz/1 1/4 cups) plain (all-purpose) flour

1 teaspoon baking powder

2 tablespoons unsweetened cocoa powder

45 g (1 1/2 oz/1/2 cup) desiccated coconut

60 g (2 1/4 oz/1/2 cup) chopped walnuts

shredded or flaked coconut, to decorate

chocolate icing (frosting)

100 g (3 1/2 oz) dark chocolate

50 g (1 3/4 oz) butter

1 tablespoon icing (confectioners') sugar

1. Preheat the oven to 180°C (350°F/Gas 4). Line a baking tray with baking paper.
2. Beat the butter and icing sugar until light and creamy. Add the egg and beat until well combined.
3. Sift the combined flour, baking powder and cocoa into a bowl. Fold into the butter mixture with the coconut and walnuts.
4. Place slightly heaped tablespoons of the mixture well apart onto the prepared tray.
5. Bake for 15–20 minutes, or until lightly browned. Leave on the tray for 5 minutes, then transfer to a wire rack to cool.
6. To make the chocolate frosting, melt the chocolate, butter and icing sugar in a small bowl set over a saucepan of simmering water. Leave to cool until the mixture has thickened, stirring occasionally.
7. Spread the frosting onto the cooled biscuits and sprinkle with the coconut while the frosting is still wet.

insy winsy spiders

MAKES 24

340 g (11¾ oz) packet chocolate cake mix
200 g (7 oz) dark chocolate
60 g (2¼ oz) butter
4 liquorice straps, for legs
48 cachous, for eyes
12 black jellybans, cut in half, for fangs
grated chocolate

1 Preheat the oven to 180°C (350°F/Gas 4). Lightly grease 24 shallow patty tins.

2 Prepare the cake mix following the directions on the packet. Fill each patty-cup two-thirds full with cake mixture.

3 Bake for 10–15 minutes. Cool on a wire rack.

4 Combine the chocolate and butter in a heatproof bowl and set over a saucepan of simmering water. Stir until mixture is smooth. Remove from heat and mix well. Set aside half of the mixture.

5 Spoon the chocolate over the cakes, ensuring that each cake is completely covered. Allow the chocolate to set.

6 Cut the liquorice straps into 10 cm (4 inch) lengths. Leave the centre uncut and cut four legs outward from the centre on both sides.

7 Glue the spider cakes on top of the legs by putting a dollop of remaining chocolate mixture on the centre patch of the legs.

8 Use cachous for the eyes. Cut jellybeans in half to make the fangs. Sprinkle cakes with grated chocolate to make furry bodies.

bat wings

MAKES 12

340 g (11¾ oz) packet chocolate cake mix

125 ml (4 fl oz/½ cup) whipped cream

2 tablespoons chocolate ice cream topping

24 red jellybeans, for eyes

1. Preheat oven to 180°C (350°F/Gas 4). Lightly grease 24 shallow patty tins and line with paper cases.
2. Prepare the cake mix following the directions on the packet. Place 1 tablespoon of mixture in each patty case.
3. Bake for 15 minutes. Cool on a wire rack.
4. Cut a round section from the top of each cake, leaving a small cavity in the cake. Cut the rounds in half.
5. Combine the whipped cream and the topping. Spoon the cream into each cavity.
6. Press half circles on top to make wing shapes. Add jellybeans for eyes.

creepy crawlies

MAKES 25

4 egg whites
230 g (8 oz/1 cup) caster (superfine) sugar
green and red food colouring
liquorice and assorted sweets, to decorate

1. Preheat the oven to 120°C (235°F/Gas 1/2). Grease two baking trays and line with baking paper.
2. Beat the egg whites in a bowl using electric beaters until soft peaks form.
3. Add the sugar gradually, beating until the mixture is thick and glossy, and the sugar has dissolved.
4. Divide the meringue mixture in half. Add a few drops of green food colouring to one bowl and a few drops of red to the other and beat.
5. Spoon each meringue mixture into a separate piping bag, fitted with a 1 cm (1/2 inch) plain, round nozzle.
6. Pipe caterpillar shapes about 8–10 cm (3 1/4–4 inch) long with the green meringue onto the trays. Pipe snail shapes with the pink meringue.
7. Decorate snails and caterpillars with assorted sweets to form features. Bake for 55–60 minutes, or until crisp. Turn off the oven but leave the meringues inside until completely cool.

maggot mounds

MAKES 30

250 g (9 oz) desiccated coconut
200 g (7 oz) condensed milk
1 teaspoon vanilla extract
glacé cherries, to decorate

1. Preheat the oven to 180°C (350°F/Gas 4). Lightly grease two baking trays.
2. Combine the coconut, condensed milk and vanilla in a bowl.
3. Drop 1 teaspoonful at a time onto the trays. Decorate the mounds with the cherries.
4. Bake for 10–12 minutes, or until lightly browned. Remove from trays and allow to cool.

green frogs

MAKES 9

- 450 g (1 lb) ready-made madeira cake
- 100 g (3½ oz) butter
- 85 g (3 oz/⅔ cup) icing (confectioners') sugar, sifted
- 2 teaspoons milk
- red food colouring
- vanilla or strawberry extract
- 9 choc melts, halved
- assorted sweets for decoration (liquorice allsorts)

icing (frosting)

- 375 g (13 oz/3 cups) icing (confectioners') sugar
- 5 tablespoons boiling water
- 2 teaspoons gelatine
- green powder, paste or liquid food colouring

1. Cut the madeira cake into three pieces lengthways. Cut each slice into three circles with a 6 cm (2½ inch) plain round cutter.
2. Beat the butter in a bowl using electric beaters until smooth. Add the icing sugar and milk and beat until light and creamy. Tint with red food colouring until pale pink and flavour with extract. Mix well.
3. Spread small mounds of mixture evenly on top of each cake round, reserving about 1 tablespoon of mixture.
4. Trim the edges of cake with a sharp knife. Attach choc melt halves to sides of cakes with reserved butter mixture.
5. Place cakes on a tray and refrigerate for 2–3 hours, or until firm.
6. To make the icing, sift the icing sugar into a bowl. Make a well in the centre. Place 2 tablespoons of the water in a small bowl. Sprinkle the gelatine on top and stir gently until dissolved. Add the mixture to remaining water. Pour onto the icing sugar and stir until smooth. Tint with green food colouring.
7. Place one cake on the flat part of a fork. Spoon the icing over the cake, allowing excess to drain back into the bowl. Transfer to a wire rack, using a knife to carefully ease cake off the fork.
8. Decorate the frogs with lollies for eyes and feet. Carefully cut out mouths with a sharp, pointed knife. Allow to set completely.

index

D

Published in 2008 by Murdoch Books Pty Limited

Murdoch Books Australia
Pier 8/9
23 Hickson Road
Millers Point NSW 2000
Phone: +61 (0) 2 8220 2000
Fax: +61 (0) 2 8220 2558
www.murdochbooks.com.au

Murdoch Books UK Limited
Erico House
6th Floor
93–99 Upper Richmond Road
Putney, London SW15 2TG
Phone: +44 (0) 20 8785 5995
Fax: +44 (0) 20 8785 5985
www.murdochbooks.co.uk

Chief Executive: Juliet Rogers
Publishing Director: Kay Scarlett

Design Manager: Vivien Valk
Design concept, art direction and design: Alex Frampton
Project Manager and Editor: Gordana Trifunovic
Production: Kita George
Photographer: Michele Aboud
Stylist: Sarah DeNardi
Food preparation: Julie Ray and Simon Ruffell

National Library of Australia Cataloguing-in-Publication Data
Broadhurst, Lucy. Ready, steady, bake. Includes index.
ISBN 978 1 74196 109 6 (pbk.)
1. Cookery—Juvenile literature. 2. Baked products. 3. Cookery (Natural foods). 4. Children's parties. I. Title. 641.5123

Printed by i-Book Printing Ltd. in 2008. PRINTED IN CHINA.

The publisher and stylist would like to thank Universal, Spotlight, Echidna Place (for clothing), Mud, and Maxwell & Williams for lending props and equipment for photography.
Many thanks to our models Isolde, Elke, Ellie, Milan, Samuel, Kai, Frankie, Eddie, Ava, Felix and Ruby.

IMPORTANT: Those who might be at risk from the effects of salmonella poisoning (the elderly, pregnant women, young children and those suffering from immune deficiency diseases) should consult their doctor with any concerns about eating raw eggs.

CONVERSION GUIDE: You may find cooking times vary depending on the oven you are using. For fan-forced ovens, as a general rule, set the oven temperature to 20°C (35°F) lower than indicated in the recipe. We have used 20 ml (4 teaspoon) tablespoon measures.